T0196052

CAISSEP.

TEACHING PROFESSIONALS

The Art of the Teaching Professional
and How to Teach Professionals
The CAISSEP® Technique

Revised AI Edition

NIGEL WILSON, PHD

ARCHWAY
PUBLISHING

Archway Publishing books may be ordered through booksellers or by contacting:

Archway Publishing
1663 Liberty Drive
Bloomington, IN 47403
www.archwaypublishing.com
844-669-3957

ISBN: 978-1-6657-0318-5 (sc)
ISBN: 978-1-6657-0319-2 (e)

Library of Congress Control Number: 2021903368

Print information available on the last page.

Archway Publishing rev. date: 03/25/2024

Better than a thousand days of diligent study is one day with a great teacher.

—Japanese proverb

The mediocre teacher tells. The good teacher explains. The superior teacher demonstrates. The great teacher inspires.

—William Arthur Ward

CONTENTS

AUTHOR

Dr Nigel Wilson is an Australian lawyer and teaching professional. He has over thirty years' experience in legal education, curriculum development, and legal practice. He was awarded a Doctor of Philosophy by the University of South Australia for his PhD thesis entitled "Regulation in the Information Age in Australia: From the Boardroom to the Courtroom". He holds degrees in Law (Honours, First Class) and Economics from the University of Adelaide and a graduate diploma in legal practice from the University of South Australia. He also holds a Master's degree in Law from Oxford University and has been awarded Harvard University's Premier Certificate in Cybersecurity.

As an expert teaching professional since 1992, Dr Wilson has been a tutor; seminar leader; examiner; course coordinator; continuing professional development presenter; convenor; senior lecturer; and director of studies of undergraduate, postgraduate, and post-admission law programmes. He has extensive experience across undergraduate and postgraduate courses, practical legal training, clinical legal practice, corporate professional development and post-admission barrister education programmes. For over three decades, he has conducted educational training programmes for Australian legal practices, workplaces, and Australian judicial colleges. Nationally and internationally, he has spoken at over sixty conferences and has twice been an invited keynote speaker at National Judicial College of Australia conferences.

From 2001 to 2008, he established and convened, pro bono, the South Australian Bar Association's (SABA) Bar Reader's Course with the SABA BRC Committee. As convenor, he designed the course curriculum, taught in the programme, and engaged with members of the courts and the profession and with national and international bars. In 2014, he was _recognised by the SABA for his teaching leadership and professionalism by the award of an annual lecture.

Dr Wilson has research expertise and has published, nationally and internationally, in legal education, the law of regulation, expert evidence, the law of evidence, competition and consumer law, insurance law, tort law, corporate law, digital forensics, risk management, cybersecurity, and technology law. He has held editorial board appointments on two leading international technology law journals and been a law reform adviser to the South Australian and Australian governments in relation to the impact of the Digital Age.

Dr Wilson has held directorships on Australian corporate boards and been a *pro bono* director of Adult Learning Australia and its charity, Learning Changes Lives, Australia's peak voice for adult learning and community education.

Since 1993, he has represented Australian and international citizens, corporations, regulators, and governments in all Australian courts and tribunals. He has also held in-house legal roles and been General Counsel of South Australia's largest private corporation and also General Counsel and Head of Governance of the Indigenous Land Corporation. He has worked extensively for, and "on country" with, indigenous Australians in complex compensation claims and indigenous rights cases.

Dr Wilson is the inventor and owner of the *CAISSEP*° teaching and learning technique.

ACKNOWLEDGEMENTS

To those by whom I have been taught, to those whom I have taught, and to those who teach—thank you.

To my partner, Dr Lydia Kovacev, parents, family, children, friends and colleagues, thank you for the gift this book seeks to illuminate.

In the development and realisation of *Teaching Professionals*, thank you to Archway Publishing and its outstanding team for their support and guidance; Darryl Bennett, Hamuck Design, for his visual design work on the CAISSEP logo and designs; Bita Forouzesh, DigiMall, for her photography; and Martin Radcliffe, *A Way with Words Business Services*, for his strategic support and insights.

Dr Nigel Wilson
Adelaide, South Australia
Tarntanya (the place of the red kangaroo)

CHAPTER 1

The Art of the Teaching Professional

The art of teaching is the art of assisting discovery.

—Mark van Doren[1]

I chose to be a teacher because I believe that education has the power to transform the society we live in. What motivates me to be a good teacher is to be an active agent in this change that is so necessary for my country, to fight against discrimination, injustice, racism, corruption and poverty. Our responsibility as teachers is enormous, and our commitment to provide quality education must be renewed every day.

—Ana, teacher, Lima, Peru[2]

Teachers are change agents. What draws us to be a teacher or motivates us to keep teaching? Are we more Ana than Mark? A blend of both? Or are we motivated by very different goals and aspirations? Whatever our motivations, this book is for each one of us.

Teachers play a key role in adult education internationally. In Australia, for example, over 3 million Australians between 15 and 64 years of age are enrolled in formal study. There are 125 registered Australian higher education providers (including 43 universities, 40 of which are

---

[1] M. Van Doren, *Liberal Education* (New York: Henry Holt, 1943).
[2] UNESCO, *Teaching and Learning: Achieving Quality for All—11ᵗʰ Education for All Global Monitoring Report* (2014), 233.

Australian, two are international and one is private). Of these institutions, 17 Australian universities are ranked in the world's top 300 universities.[3]

However, towering over these figures, illiteracy among adults internationally remains "stubbornly high" at over 770 million people, with women making up almost two-thirds of this number.[4]

Meaningful and engaging teaching and learning skills are at the core of the adult learning system and are the avenue for improvements in literacy worldwide. Motivated and motivational teachers are its lifeblood. To improve literacy levels and enhance opportunity through the sharing of knowledge and skills, adult education is a key driver for change—globally. As positive as the current teaching outcomes are for Australia, and for other first world countries, there is a vast international teaching challenge and there exists an educational divide.

Wherever teaching occurs, it is both an opportunity and a responsibility which requires a professional approach. To this end, this book proposes the CAISSEP technique of teaching and learning, with both clarity of purpose and professionalism at its heart.

Teaching is many things—a career, a profession, a calling, a vocation, and a gift. Teaching is both practical and theoretical. Teaching can also be filled with wonder—the "Eureka" or "aha" moment when a student achieves understanding or makes a discovery.[5] In these emotion-filled experiences, the reward of teaching is captured. It has been described, accurately, in this way:

> I am a teacher at heart, and there are moments in the classroom when I can hardly hold the joy. When my students and I discover unchartered territory to explore, when the pathway out of a thicket opens up before us, when our experience is illumined by the lightning-life of the mind – then teaching is the finest work I know.[6]

The title of this book, *Teaching Professionals*, is deliberate. On the one hand, using the word *teaching* as an adjective, its intended audience is professional teachers—now often referred to as teaching professionals, teaching experts, or teaching specialists. It is to the art of teaching for the teaching professional that this book is dedicated. On the other hand, using *teaching* as a verb, its further intended audience is those teachers who teach professionals. For example, it is intended for those who teach undergraduate and postgraduate students who aspire to become professionals,

---

[3] Australian Trade and Investment Commission, *Australian Education Technology—Education of the Future Now*, (Commonwealth of Australia, 2016), 27.

[4] UNESCO, *Teaching and Learning*, 4.

[5] H. Wong and R. Wong, *The First Days of School—How to be an effective Teacher* (5th edn, Harry K Wong Publications Inc., 2018).

[6] P. Palmer, *The Courage to Teach—Exploring the Inner Landscape of the Teacher's Life* (Jossey-Bass, 2007), 1.

but it is also for those who teach in continuous learning programmes, in compulsory professional development courses, in postgraduate training, and in lifelong learning.

Besides its joy, the teaching of professionals is challenging and complex. It is well recognised that teaching is "a highly complex psychosocial drama in which the personalities of the individuals involved, the contextual setting for the educational transaction, and the prevailing political climate crucially affect the nature and form of learning."[7] Through the application of the CAISSEP technique, these challenges can be identified and diminished.

As the expression is commonly understood, "professionals" have or are learning specialised knowledge. The teaching of professionals requires teachers to impart their expertise. In the law context, experts who are called to give evidence in trials play a highly influential role in cases and their outcomes. It has been said that the expert must not only be learned in the field but must also be able to give meaningful explanations. He or she must be an effective communicator: "Their function is to educate the court in the technology—they come as teachers, as makers of the mantle for the court to don. For that purpose it does not matter whether they do or do not approximate to the skilled man. What matters is how good they are at explaining things."[8]

It has been said that teaching is to be delivered neutrally or "value free," but this approach is disconnected from the original meaning of professional—someone who is motivated by a "profession of faith".[9] With a greater emphasis on emotional intelligence and its drivers, of both teachers and students, the teaching of professionals can be highly fulfilling, sustaining, and empowering.[10]

Teaching is also a creative process. For example, it has been said that legal education "does not differ in this respect from any other human endeavour that is truly creative.[11] However, creativity takes courage.[12] So does teaching, but with the potential for remarkable results: "Let us remember: One book, one pen, one child, and one teacher can change the world. Education is the only solution. Education first."[13]

As with teaching, this book does not seek to suggest all of the answers. It's intended to provide guidance, to challenge, and to inform. It's intended to stimulate your desire to improve your craft

---

[7] S. Brookfield, *Understanding and Facilitating Adult Learning*, (Jossey-Bass, 1991), vii.

[8] *Rockwater* v. *Technip France SA & Ors* [2004] EWCA Civ 381, per Lord Justice Jacob.

[9] Palmer, *The Courage to Teach*, 212.

[10] Palmer, *The Courage to Teach*, 205–12.

[11] L. Fuller, "On Teaching Law", *Stanford Law Review*, 3 (1950–1951) 35.

[12] H. Matisse, 1869–1954.

[13] M. Yousafzai and C. Lamb. *I Am Malala: The Girl Who Stood up for Education and Was Shot by the Taliban* (Little Brown & Company, 2013). Malala Yousafzai is the youngest Nobel Peace Prize recipient.

and develop your art (and science)[14] of teaching. It is through your journey that you will add new chapters and subtopics. The experiences of the author and the guidance provided in this book are drawn from a shared and sharing community of teachers, researchers, and students. There is no intention in this book either to monopolise our understanding of the art or science of teaching or to suggest that the author has such a monopoly. Yet, through teaching, there are many mysteries to discover if we are willing to be adventurous and to open our eyes. This concept is so simply expressed by one of history's greatest scientists, who commenced his career as a lecturer and became a professor: "The most beautiful thing we can experience is the mysterious. It is the source of all true art and all science. He to whom this emotion is a stranger, who can no longer pause to wonder and stand rapt in awe, is as good as dead: his eyes are closed" (Albert Einstein).

Teaching also requires a combination of agility, patience, and versatility, as well as consistency, innovation, and pastoral care in an unstable world.

With the advent of the coronavirus pandemic in 2020, teaching across all disciplines and in all domains has been adversely impacted by the largest disruption to education systems in history—nearly 1.6 billion students in more than 190 countries and across every continent have been affected.[15]

In an attempt to provide continuity in teaching, new teaching environments have evolved or become more fully developed—for example, in the "student-free" classroom and the "teacher-less" lecture hall. As a result, the education experience has changed for all, social interactions have been constrained, social distancing has been enforced as a matter of government policy, and learning and teaching have been conducted from and in homes and domestic settings. Teaching institutions have themselves been closed, some permanently, and students and teachers alike have been affected by illness and death. Educational experiences, evaluations, outcomes, and student and teacher well-being have been changed forever. Where existing, and often longstanding, "digital divides" exist, technological solutions are hopelessly limited and are often unavailable due to lack of access to modern technologies and sufficient resources for educational platforms and infrastructure.

The pandemic has created a social and economic crisis. Learning itself has been threatened. The United Nations has observed:

---

[14] Greer emphasises the "science" of teaching, as opposed to the "art" on the basis that *"teaching as a strategic science* determines the rate of student progress" in D. Greer, *Designing Teaching Strategies: An Applied Behaviour Analysis Systems Approach* (Academic Press: Elsevier Science, 2002), xv–xvi. See also the analysis in the chapter "The Paradigm Problem" in G. Squires, *Teaching as a Professional Discipline*, (Falmer Press, 1999) regarding the paradigms of teaching. The Suggested teaching paradigms are that it is at least a common-sense activity, an art, a craft, an applied science, a system, a reflective practice and a matter of competence but also that it is a professional activity.

[15] United Nations, *Education During COVID-19 and Beyond, Policy Brief* (August 2020), 2.

The crisis is exacerbating pre-existing education disparities by reducing the opportunities for many of the most vulnerable children, youth, and adults—those living in poor or rural areas, girls, refugees, persons with disabilities and forcibly displaced persons—to continue their learning. Learning losses also threaten to extend beyond this generation and erase decades of progress, not least in support of girls and young women's educational access and retention. Some 23.8 million additional children and youth (from pre-primary to tertiary) may drop out or not have access to school next year due to the pandemic's economic impact alone.[16]

The United Nations has made an urgent call to all of us to *reimagine education* and to *accelerate change* in teaching and learning, in order to prevent "a learning crisis from becoming a generational catastrophe."[17]

In parallel with the challenges of the pandemic, teaching has been confronted by exciting, but also threatening, technological developments including 'Artificial Intelligence' (commonly referred to as 'AI')! AI builds on diverse, modern technologies which have impacted, and radically changed, teaching methodologies and learning domains. The United Nations has cautiously emphasised that the "growing use of novel AI technologies in education will only benefit all of humanity if – by design – it enhances human-centred approaches to pedagogy, and respects ethical norms and standards."[18]

In this revised edition, enhancements to CAISSEP's human-centric teaching and learning techniques have been added to assist and guide teaching with new technologies, including AI!

It is the author's modest hope that, with commitment and care but with fewer resources at hand, this book and its techniques may provide positive, practical resources to assist teachers to reimagine and accelerate human-centric change for today's and future generations.

---

[16] United Nations, *Education During COVID-19*, 2.
[17] United Nations, *Education During COVID-19*, 3–4.
[18] United Nations, *AI and education – Guidance for policy-makers*, (2021), 2

CHAPTER 2

Experiential Learning for Teaching Professionals

2.1. What Is So Special about Adult Learning?

This book is directed to adult learning. Adults need to be taught differently from children. Knowles,[19] one of the early adult learning specialists, identified several key principles for effective adult learning:

1. Self-directed—motivation is developed by *why* the student is learning.
2. Learning happens by doing in the student's *own way* through different techniques, which includes
   a. *visual*, with an emphasis on the need to be *shown*;
   b. *auditory*, with an emphasis on the need to be *told*; and
   c. *kinaesthetic*, or *tactile*, with an emphasis on the need to *do*.
3. Respect and encouragement are included.
4. Experiential learning is based on real life and the student's own experience.

The "science" of teaching has been a rich source of research in recent generations, and it has been highly influenced by Kolb's Experiential Learning Cycle (see figure 2.1).[20]

---

[19] Malcolm Knowles, *The Adult Learner: A Neglected Species* (Houston: Gulf Publishing, 1973). Knowles is often cited as the key developer of *andragogy*—an expression first used by Kapp in 1883 in relation to teaching practices and theories for adult learning.

[20] D. Kolb, *Experiential Learning—Experience as the Source of Learning and Development* (Prentice-Hall, New Jersey, 1984).

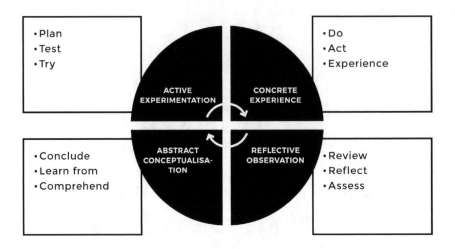

Figure 2.1. Kolb's Experiential Learning Cycle

Experiential learning emphasises[21] *both* the student's *and* the teacher's perspectives. From a *learning perspective*, students are encouraged to be involved in:

1. active exploration;
2. testing assumptions and ideas;
3. critical reflection;
4. a course, programme, or task that matters to them and that they are open to learning;
5. an independent and autonomous inquiry; and
6. trusting themselves to participate in the process and their own experience and conclusions.

From a *teaching perspective,* teachers are encouraged to:

1. develop, design, structure and review "experiential" exercises and programmes;
2. facilitate reflection by students and the teacher; and
3. facilitate safe and supportive environments for learning.

---

[21] G. Gibbs, *Learning by Doing* (Oxford Centre for Staff and Learning Development, 2013), 19–20. The concept of "phenomenography" is drawn from clinical psychology and captures the concept that it is the learner's perspective that determines or influences what is learned, rather than what the teacher considers should be learned. The concept of "constructivism", again drawn from clinical psychology, encapsulates the concept that students "construct" knowledge through activities and by building on their own prior knowledge. J. Biggs and C. Tang, *Teaching for Quality Learning at University* (3rd edn, McGraw Hill, 2007), 20–21.

Importantly, increasing emphasis has been placed on facilitating, helping, nurturing, and supporting students[22] and, in particular, on ensuring a safe teaching environment. However, it has been said that, of these, it is reflection that is "the magic ingredient"[23] that converts experience into education.

When these elements are present and are combined with the motivational drivers for adult learning—need to know, readiness to learn, and an orientation towards learning[24]—an environment for effective learning is ripe. In that learning domain, the role of the teacher is to act as a guide and facilitator.

2.2. Connection, Communication, and Community

Whether it is with friends, family, work colleagues, or new acquaintances, there are some key fundamentals to connecting effectively. Shorn of their detail,[25] they include:

1. communication
2. usefulness
3. relevance
4. safety
5. engagement
6. respect

But communication itself does not always lead to information retention or skills transfer. As with our life experiences, different teaching methods lead to more effective retention and skills development. As Dale's highly influential, but sometimes controversial, Cone of Learning seeks to illustrate, recollection is said to be enhanced by active participation, rather than simply by passive observation. Despite its seeming levels of accuracy, Dale emphasised that the cone is but a "visual model, a pictorial device that may help you think critically about the ways in which concepts are developed".[26]

---

[22] Australian Government Office for Learning and Teaching, *Australian University Teaching Criteria and Standards Framework* (hereafter Australian Universities Teaching Criteria), Teaching Criteria 2 (2020).

[23] G. Ledvinka, "Reflection and Assessment in Clinical Legal Education: Do You See What I See?" *International Journal of Clinical Legal Education*, 29 (2006), 29–30.

[24] Knowles, *The Adult Learner*.

[25] Knowles, *The Adult Learner*.

[26] P. Dale, *Audiovisual Methods in Teaching* (3rd edn, Holt, Rinehart and Winston, 1969).

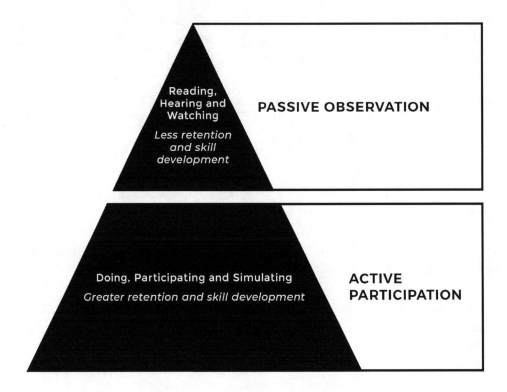

Figure 2.2. Dale's Cone of Learning (simplified by Dr Nigel Wilson)

In a school, a college, a faculty or a workplace, the fostering of a community is beneficial to the development of a sense of belonging. A sense of belonging has a positive impact on the learning environment as "a growing body of research confirms the benefits of building a sense of community … students with a strong sense of community are more likely to be academically motivated."[27]

How we communicate and the community we build are central to effective teaching. Often overlooked, these elements are over and above standard teaching techniques. They go to the question of who we are and how we see ourselves as teachers. In doing so, they define us, our identity, and our personality. They provide the stimulus that motivates us to teach and spurs us on to teach with

---

[27] E. Schaps, "Creating a School Community", *Educational Leadership*, 60 (2003), 31, 33; B. Davis, *Tools for Teaching* (Jossey-Bass Publishers, 1993), 726. Quality education, through the careful weaving of cultural knowledge into curriculum is "governed by strong collaborators among teachers and the community"; N. Harrison and J. Sellwood, *"Learning and Teaching in Aboriginal and Torres Strait Islander Education"* (Oxford University Press, 4th Edition,2022), 179.

passion. It has been insightfully observed that "good teaching cannot be reduced to technique; good teaching comes from the identity and integrity of the teacher."[28]

As teaching professionals, we draw on diverse teaching techniques, our own identity, and our integrity on a daily basis to teach professionally. This book will provide skills, techniques, and insights, from planning and preparation to teaching with technology. At its core, each chapter will emphasise the key elements of the CAISSEP technique.

Review of Chapter 2	
Having read this chapter, you will be able to do the following:	
1	Identify the key principles of effective adult learning
2	Identify the four elements of experiential learning
3	Describe how to encourage both *learner* and *teacher* perspectives in experiential learning
4	Describe effective communication techniques to enhance information retention
5	Describe the role of one's teaching identity and of integrity in good teaching

---

[28] Palmer, *The Courage to Teach*, 10.

CHAPTER 3

Introducing the CAISSEP Technique

Those who know, do. Those that understand, teach.

—Aristotle

3.1 Learning Objectives

What do students need to learn? This is the starting point in the preparation of any subject, lecture, seminar, tutorial, programme, or degree or their sub-components. Learning objectives should be identified and documented and be drawn, predominantly, from the student's perspective. Mager's[29] three questions for learning objectives are an invaluable guide to course/teaching planning:

1. What will students be *competent* at when they complete the course?
2. What are the *conditions* in which students will perform or undertake the activities in the course?
3. What *level of competency* is expected of students to perform the course tasks?

3.2. Teaching Standards

Across all disciplines, teaching standards have also come to the fore in parallel with developments regarding learning objectives. In most areas, these standards seek to address (a) course content and

---

[29] R. Mager, *Preparing Instructional Objectives: A Critical Tool in the Development of Effective Instruction*, (3rd edn, Center for Effective Performance, 1997).

threshold learning outcomes, (b) assessment standards, (c) grievance standards, and (d) academic integrity requirements. Beyond these, particularly in the context of teaching professionals, additional standards apply to ensure consistency. In their preparation, extensive consultation is often necessary with peak bodies, students, academics, and regulators.[30] In professional programmes, such as law, medicine, commerce, engineering, or architecture, liaison and approval is required from courts, specialist colleges, professional institutions, or academies, respectively.

In Australian universities,[31] seven core teaching criteria have been identified:

1. design and planning of learning activities
2. teaching and supporting student learning
3. assessment and giving feedback to students on their learning
4. developing effective learning environments, student support, and guidance
5. integration of scholarship, research, and professional activities with teaching and in support of student learning
6. evaluation of practice and continuing professional development
7. professional and personal effectiveness.

Within the parameters of these standards and criteria, there are numerous opportunities and possibilities. Good standards and criteria should create good teaching environments[32] and good learning outcomes and facilitate moments of discovery. It is vital to approach our role as teachers with professionalism[33] and a positive perspective about its intrinsic capacity to inspire and motivate not just learning but also change:

> The academy is not paradise. But learning is a place where paradise can be created. The classroom, with all its limitations, remains a location of possibility. In that field of possibility we have the opportunity to labor for freedom, to demand of ourselves and our comrades, an openness of mind and heart that allows us to face reality even as we collectively imagine ways to move beyond boundaries, to transgress. This is education as the practice of freedom.[34]

---

[30] In Australia, the Tertiary Education Quality and Standards Agency is an independent standards regulator.

[31] Australian Government Office for Learning and Teaching, *Australian Universities Teaching Criteria*.

[32] Australian Government Office for Learning and Teaching, *Australian Universities Teaching Criteria*, Criteria 4.

[33] Australian Government Office for Learning and Teaching, *Australian Universities Teaching Criteria*, Criteria 7.

[34] B. Hooks, *Teaching to Transgress: Education as the Practice of Freedom* (Routledge, 1994), 207.

3.3 Teaching and Learning Outcomes and Activities

The development of outcomes-based teaching in the late twentieth and early twenty-first centuries has sought to fulfil diverse goals—(a) standardisation, (b) benchmarking, (c) accountability, and (d) managerial control.[35] At their core, teaching and learning outcomes (TLOs) and teaching/learning activities (TLAs) are intended to provide focus—focus on what the *student* is to learn, rather than on the topics to be taught. The TLOs are descriptive of the teaching/learning activity (TLA) that is to be undertaken and inform students what they're expected to learn. Finally, the TLAs should be linked to the assessment tasks (ATs).[36]

An approach that places emphasis on the outputs of the instruction given and its purposes has been described as "backward design".[37] It is said to contrast with conventional "forward design" methodologies, which approach the design process sequentially—starting with its content (for example, learning activities); moving to assessments; and then seeking to draw linkages to learning goals. The backward design approach seeks to emphasise transparency in curriculum design and the preparation of learning activities.

In the preparation of TLOs and TLAs, it is accepted practice to adopt the language of Bloom's revised taxonomy,[38] which is a dynamic ordering of cognitive skills and educational goals.

---

[35] Biggs and Tang, *Teaching for Quality Learning*, 2–14.

[36] Biggs and Tang, *Teaching for Quality Learning*, 52; Australian Government Office for Learning and Teaching, *Australian Universities Teaching Criteria*, Criteria 3.

[37] G. Wiggins and J. McTighe, *Understanding by Design* (Association for Supervision and Curriculum Development, 1998).

[38] L. Anderson and D. Krathwohl, eds. *A Taxonomy for Learning, Teaching, and Assessing: A Revision of Bloom's Taxonomy of Educational Objectives* (complete edition, New York: Longman, 2001).

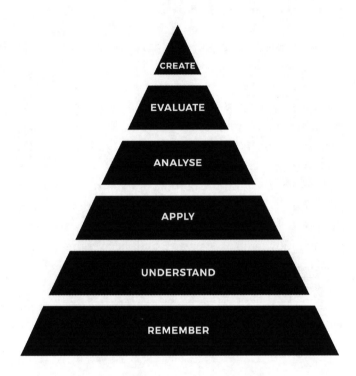

Figure 3.1. Bloom's Taxonomy

3.4 Practical Teaching Techniques

A variety of practical teaching techniques for effective learning has been formulated over time:

Technique	Approach	Developed by
Think-Pair-Share	*Think*—of an answer individually to a question arising from an exercise *Pair*—students pair up *Share*—students share their answers, with volunteers sought from the class	Lyman[38]
Think-Write–Pair-Share	As above, but with written answers prepared individually by students	
Read-Write-Pair-Share	As above, but with the exercise being read individually by students	Fisher, et al.[39]
Tell-Help-Check	Students are numbered (1s or 2s). *Tell*—1s, e.g., are selected to answer a problem *Help*—2s, e.g., are requested to help by adding or editing information in the answer *Check*—1s and 2s then check the answer	Archer and Gleeson[40]
Problem-Based Learning	Students actively solve complex and challenging problems	Barrows and Tamblyn[41] and others[42]
MIRAT	Analysis based upon: M—material facts I—issues R—rules and resources A—arguments and application T—tentative conclusion	Wade[43]

Figure 3.2. Practical Teaching Techniques and Approaches

[39] F. Lyman, "Think-Pair-Share: An Expanding Teaching Technique", *MAA-CIE Cooperative News*, 1 (1987), 1–2.

[40] D. Fisher, et al., *Content Area Strategies for Adolescent Literacy* (Pearson, 2007).

[41] A. Archer and M. Gleeson, *Skills for School Success* (Book 6, Curriculum Associates, 1994).

[42] H. Barrows and R. Tamblyn, *Problem-Based Learning: An Approach to Medical Education* (Springer, 1980).

[43] See the scholars and scholarship in notes 41–48.

[44] J. Wade, "Meet MIRAT: Legal Reasoning Fragmented into Learnable Chunks" *Legal Education Review*, 2 (1990–91), 283.

Problem-based learning (PBL) was introduced over fifty years ago in a Canadian medical school. Since then, it has been applied across the world in most disciplines.

In its original form, the creator of problem-based learning, Professor Howard Barrows, emphasised:

1. student focus,
2. small groups,
3. facilitation-based guidance,
4. problems as the basis and stimulus for learning,
5. the development of problem-solving skills, and
6. self-direction in its approach to new knowledge.

From a student perspective, it's recommended that problem-based curriculum is:[45]

1. cumulative,
2. integrated,
3. progressive, and
4. consistent.

In further developments on PBL, emphasis has been placed on strategy,[46] critical thinking,[47] the analysis and resolution of complex and messy real-world problems,[48] and the integration of computer-based education modules.[49] The absence of a single correct answer to the problem under consideration has also been promoted. Further derivatives also include *project*-based learning and *inquiry* -based learning.

More advanced PBL-teaching seeks to achieve a smoother transition in the delivery of information from the "knowledge bank" through the "information provider" by the adoption of the "learning facilitator"[50] technique. More recently, increased benefits are said to arise from transparent teaching

---

[45] J. Leach and B. Moon, *Learners and Pedagogy* (Paul Chapman Publishing, 1999), 206.

[46] D. Boud and G. Feletti, *The Challenge of Problem-Based Learning* (2nd edn, London: Kogan Page, 1997).

[47] B. Duch, S. Groh, and D. Allen, eds., *The Power of Problem-Based Learning* (Sterling, VA: Stylus, 2001).

[48] L. Torp and S. Sage, *Problems as Possibilities: Problem-Based Learning for K-16 Education* (2nd edn, Alexandria, VA: Association for Supervision and Curriculum Development, 2002).

[49] F. Martin, "Teaching Legal Problem Solving: A Problem-Based Learning Approach Combined with a Computerised Generic Problem", *Legal Education Review* (2003), 77.

[50] J. Savery, "Overview of PBL: Definitions and Distinctions" *Interdisciplinary Journal of Problem-based Learning* (2006), 9.

through the sharing of data, particularly for under-represented and first-generation university students.[51]

"Design-thinking" teaching involves students in the preparation, prototype design, presentation and appraisal of projects to enhance their learning experience, creativity and interdisciplinary collaboration and to provide "all-encompassing" experiential learning.[52]

3.5 Teaching Styles: Developing Your Own

"Teaching skills can be taught or, often, learned by experience—sink or swim."[53] From the moment a teacher steps in front of the class, she or he is on stage.[54] Teachers bring their skills to their craft. A key element of successful teaching is to know your audience and to develop your own style.

Various teaching styles[55] include:

> **Lecturer**. Lecturer style is "teacher-centred" and is often authoritarian, one-directional, and with little interaction. Students are passive and absorb information.

> **Demonstrator**. Similar to the lecturer, the demonstrator demonstrates to students the information they need to absorb.

> **Facilitator**. The facilitator encourages self-learning and discovery. By way of student participation and task management, the facilitator encourages critical thinking through tailored feedback.

> **Coordinator**. The coordinator guides and observes students and imposes less authority on the learning environment. The coordinator often utilises group learning and delegates roles to groups.

---

[51] M. Winkelmes, "Transparency in Teaching: Faculty Share Data and Improve Students' Learning" *Liberal Education*, 99 (2013), 2.

[52] R. Hews and Ors, "Creative confidence and thinking skills for lawyers: Making sense of design thinking pedagogy in legal education", *Thinking Skills and Creativity* (2023), 2.

[53] D. Whaley, "Teaching Law: Advice for the New Professor", *Ohio St. Law Journal*, 42 (1982), 125.

[54] S. Schwartz and B. Karge, *Human Diversity: A Guide for Understanding* (New York: McGraw-Hill, 1996).

[55] R. Boyle and R. Dunn, "Teaching Law Students through Individual Learning Styles" *Alberta Law Review*, 62 (1998–1999), 213.

Composite. The composite blends teaching styles depending on the subject, student needs, and learning exercises.

Every student is different, and each has a different learning style, pace, and approach. Whilst classifying students can lead to over-generalisations, four recognised learning styles[56] can be found in figure 3.3.

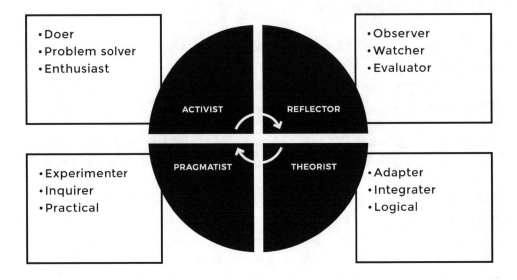

Figure 3.3. Four Recognised Learning Styles

The style dimensions derived when Kolb's experiential learning criteria are overlaid on the above learning styles are shown in figure 3.3.

---

[56] P. Honey and A. Mumford, *The Manual of Learning Styles* (Peter Honey Associates, 1986).

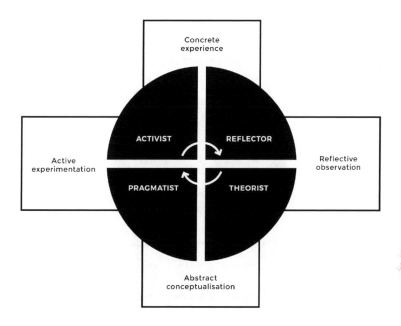

Figure 3.4. Four Recognised Learning Styles with Kolb's Experiential Learning Criteria

3.6. The CAISSEP Technique

CAISSEP, developed by the author, builds on the established experiential adult learning and problem-based learning traditions and their derivatives, through the methodical development of innovative curricula, course materials, integrated assessments, and teaching methodologies. CAISSEP is an acronym for the following teaching and learning techniques:

Clarity
Analysis
Inquiry
System
Structure
Emphasis
Professional

CAISSEP is also a simple play on words. The French word *caisse* means "box" or "case", and its etymology is drawn from the Latin word *capsa*, which also means "box", "case", or "repository". In that sense, CAISSEP is both a learning and teaching technique and a toolbox (of information, tools, or techniques), with the addition of the key final letter—*P* for professional! Embedded within CAISSEP, both the acronym and its techniques, is the potential for the effective use of AI – C**AI**SSEP!

The central elements of the CAISSEP technique, each fully supported by the research and scholarship of learning and teaching, are as follows:

Clarity.[57] Easy to comprehend teaching and learning techniques that are readily apparent, distinctive, and explanatory of their content, tasks, and assessments.

Style. Clear, open, transparent, explanatory.

---

[57] N. Hativa, *Clarity in Teaching: Importance and Components, Teaching for Effective Learning in Higher Education* (Springer, 2000).

Analysis.[58] Active, analytical investigation of problems, issues, and trends.

Style. Active, argument-based, experiential, solution-based including critical analysis, issue identification, advice and judgement.

---

[58] Also called cognitive task analysis. G. Velmahos, et al., "Cognitive Task Analysis for Teaching Technical Skills in an Inanimate Surgical Skills Laboratory", *The American Journal of Surgery*, 187 (2004), 114.

CAISSEP. INQUIRY

Inquiry[59] Relevant, inquisitive questioning based on self-directed learning and discovery.

Style. Autonomous, inquiring, eager for knowledge, involved.

---

[59] A. King, "Changing College Classrooms: New Teaching and Learning Strategies for an Increasingly Complex World", chapter 2 in *Inquiry as a Tool in Critical Thinking*, D. Halpern D, ed., (Jossey-Bass, 1994). Question and answer lie "at the heart of the processes of explaining and exploring"; G. Squires, *Teaching as a Professional Discipline*, (Falmer Press, 1999), p.98

System.[60] Orderly provision of information and data, which is based on principles, categories and precedent.

Style. In-depth, detailed, informative, astute, discriminating.

---

[60] V. Clarke and V. Braun, "Teaching Thematic Analysis: Overcoming Challenges and Developing Strategies for Effective Learning", *Psychologist*, 26 (2013), 120.

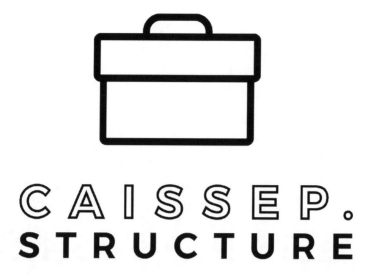

Structure.[61] Relevant, balanced, logical consideration of issues by the use of consistent, organised frameworks and methodical approaches.

Style. Reflective, analytical, organised, planned.

---

[61] R. Bruner, "Repetition is the First Principle of All Learning", *Psychology* (2001); K. Saville, "Strategies for Using Repetition as a Powerful Teaching Tool", *Music Educators Journal*, 98 (2011), 69.

Emphasis[62] Clear highlighting of foundational issues, concepts, and principles.

Style. Emphatic, critical, focused, challenging, impactful.

---

[62]   D. Carr, *Professionalism and Ethics in Teaching* (Routledge, 1999); H. Fehring and S. Rodrigues, eds., *Teaching, Coaching and Mentoring Adult Learners: Lessons for Professionalism and Partnership* (New York: Routledge, 2017). G. Squires, *Teaching as a Professional Discipline*, (Falmer Press, 1999) p. 86 adopts the expression "reinforce".

CAISSEP.
PROFESSIONAL

Professional.[63] Emphasis on professional and ethical considerations integrated with reflective awareness.

Style. Professional, ethical, considered, fair, just, reflective.

The CAISSEP symbols can be readily used in teaching materials, and students can be informed of their meaning. Alternatively, they can be used behind the scenes in curriculum and course development as aids to prompt, or as reminders of the need for, the inclusion of each of the techniques to ensure the necessary variation, balance, and points of emphasis for the learning environment.

Finally, the style keywords are from both a teacher-delivery and student-engagement perspective. Certain teaching materials or content will more naturally align with particular styles. However, role play can facilitate deeper learning, and by making adjustments in teaching style and learning modes, the learning environment can be modulated and enriched.

---

[63] Carr, *Professionalism and Ethics*; Fehring and Rodrigues, *Teaching, Coaching and Mentoring*.

3.7. The CAISSEP Technique in the "Flipped" Classroom

The traditional "lecture" format has often been heavily tied to the formal delivery of content. "Flipping the classroom" teaching strategies seek to externalise some learning by students so that it is undertaken outside the classroom. This is done to ensure greater student preparation and to enable more dynamic and interactive lectures or classes to be held. Pre-reading, with guidance, by students of materials enables key concepts or principles to be presented and discussed (individually or collaboratively) in class, often at greater depth.[64]

In the "flipped" classroom, the teacher acts as a facilitator—sometimes described as a "guide on the side", rather than a "sage on the stage".[65] The CAISSEP technique, with its emphasis on problem-solving, inquiry, analysis, and professionalism, is readily applied in the flipped classroom, including when it is conducted virtually. The "flipped" classroom (together with Bloom's Taxonomy) is outlined in figure 3.5.

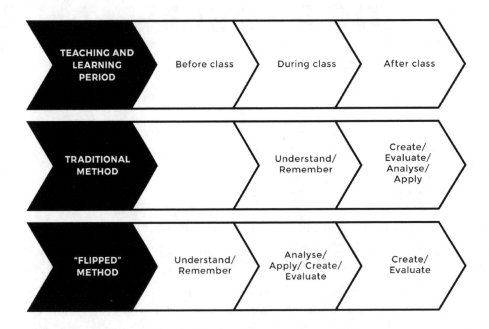

Figure 3.5. The Flipped Classroom with Bloom's Taxonomy

---

[64] L. Gomes and P. Anselm, *Scaffolding Learning and Maximising Engagement*, https://learningandteaching-navitas.com/scaffolding-learning-maximising-engagement/.

[65] King, "Changing College Classrooms".

3.8 Planning:[66] The Role of the Teaching Plan and Integrated Assessments

Once the framework for the topic is set (whether by forward design or reverse design), individual teaching plans should be prepared. Teaching plans should flow from (and be linked to) the overarching framework—the teaching learning outcomes, teaching and learning activities, and the assessment tasks.

Teaching plans are invaluable to:

1.   provide consistency;
2.   focus on (a) learning outcomes, (b) activities/tasks, (c) timing, and (d) format;
3.   ensure clarity of the learning journey for students;
4.   assist teacher reflection;
5.   improve teaching confidence through control and direction;
6.   assist the ability to share;
7.   record performance and impact;[67] and
8.   identify technologies, including AI, to be used.

Assessments play a key role in adult education[68] but are said to be "one of the most controversial issues in higher education today".[69] What are their purposes? A functional approach is to say that assessments are "the process of defining, selecting, designing, collecting, analysing, interpreting and using information to increase students' learning and development."[70] More broadly, the United Kingdom Quality Assurance Agency has identified four purposes for assessment:[71]

- *Pedagogy*—promoting student learning by providing feedback to help the student improve (and also to determine what and how students learn)

---

[66] Australian Government Office for Learning and Teaching, *Australian Universities Teaching Criteria*, 1.

[67] L. Gomes and G. Lowe, https://learningandteaching-navitas.com/8-reasons-start-using-lesson-plans-2/.

[68] General approaches to assessments (and their interrelationship with learning activities) are considered throughout this book and are addressed, specifically in the clarity element of the CAISSEP technique. Due to their diversity, specific approaches to assessment, often the subject of faculty or regulated requirements, are not addressed in this book.

[69] L. Norton, "Assessing Student learning", in *A Handbook for Teaching and Learning* in H. Fry, et al., *Higher Education: Enhancing Academic Practice* (3rd edn, Routledge, 2009), 132; G. Davis and S. Owen, *Innovation Is Afoot: Some Innovations in Assessment in Legal Education* (Council of Australian Law Deans, 2009).

[70] W. Sullivan, et al., *Educating Lawyers*, (2007, Jossey-Bass).

[71] Quality Assurance Agency, *Code of Practice for the Assurance of Academic Quality and Standards in Higher Education* (2nd edn, 2006), 4.

- *Measurement*—evaluating student knowledge, understanding, abilities or skills
- *Standardisation*—marking or grading to enable the establishment of a student's performance level
- *Certification*—enabling the public and employers to know an individual has reached a level of achievement.

Forms and methods of assessment are as diverse as the disciplines taught in adult education.[72] A distinction is drawn between *formative* assessment, which identifies how a student is progressing and provides feedback, and *summative* assessment, an assessment that contributes to a grade (and also enables feedback to be given).

In designing integrated curricula and assessments, issues to be addressed include:

a. the subject matter of the assessment—content, problem, competency, skills
b. the type of assessment format—exam (closed-book, open-book, take-home); essay or report; portfolio; quiz (multiple choice, short answer etc.); individual or group project; simulation; clinic/work placement; field trip; laboratory practical; advocacy exercise; presentation (oral, video, poster presentation, viva voce)
c. the weighting of the assessment
d. the marking scale and process—pass/fail, pass to high distinction, ungraded pass, resubmission and remarking
e. the transparency levels of the assessment—criteria, rubrics, and prerequisites
f. marker responsibility—teacher, computer-aided, peer-assessment, self-assessment, internal marker (not the teacher) or external
g. plagiarism detection and its consequences.

Based on the CAISSEP teaching technique, a suggested but easily varied teaching plan for a teaching session (a lecture or seminar, for example) that integrates with relevant assessments could include: (1) overview; (2) pre-class, class and post-class content and activities; (3) linkages to objectives, learning outcomes, and assessments; (4) teaching aids (including technology and AI); and (5) reflections and recommendations for change (see figure 3.6).

---

[72] See A. Bates, *Teaching in a Digital Age* (Tony Bates Associates Ltd, 2015); L. Earle, *Assessment as Learning* (Thousand Oaks: Corwin Press, 2003); G. Gibbs, "Using Assessment Strategically to Change the Way Students Learn", in S. Brown and A. Glasner, eds., *Assessment Matters in Higher Education* (Open University Press, 1999).

CAISSEP Teaching Plan
(Including Pre- and Post-Class Content and Reflection)

Overview	Teacher:	Date: Time:
Location		
Course		
Module/Session		
Objectives / Learning Outcomes		
Teaching Aids (including technology and AI)		
No. of Students		

Pre-Class		Summary of Tasks/Activities

Class Content	Time	Summary of Tasks/Activities	
Introduction			
Gain attention			
Link to/ recap prior knowledge			
Share session learning objectives/ purpose			
Body	**Time**	**Summary of Sessions/Tasks/Activities (inc. feedback and practical issues)**	**Teaching Aids**
		Break	
Conclusions			
Outcomes			
Feedback			
Assessments (if applicable)			
Future			

Post-Class		Summary of Tasks/Activities	
Reflection / Recommended Changes			Dr Nigel Wilson, CAISSEP, 2024

Figure 3.6. CAISSEP Teaching Plan

Whatever your teaching style, it should be developed purposefully with both integrity and professionalism. As the teaching plan suggests, an introduction—of yourself, the subject, and the lesson—should be given at the start of the session. By sharing, an environment of trust can be built and a platform for reflective learning can be developed: "Professors who established a special trust with their students often displayed the kind of openness in which they might, from time to time, talk about their intellectual journey, its ambitions, triumphs, frustrations, and failures, and encourage students to be similarly reflective and candid."[73]

The CAISSEP technique encourages the use of a variety of teaching styles for a variety of student learning styles. With practice and the use of the CAISSEP techniques, confidence will be gained with different styles and in varied audiences and in diverse subjects.

Review of chapter 3 Having read this chapter, you will be able to:	
1	Identify three questions for learning objectives
2	Describe three practical teaching techniques
3	Describe the benefits of the "flipped" classroom
4	Describe the elements of the CAISSEP technique
5	Prepare a teaching plan using the CAISSEP template

---

[73] K. Bain, *What the Best College Teachers Do* (Harvard University Press, 2004), chapter 6.

CHAPTER 4

Teaching Small Groups

*Teachers have three loves: love of learning, love of learners, and
the love of bringing the first two loves together.*

—Scott Hayden

4.1. From the Tutorial to the Seminar

Many skills and crafts can only be taught effectively one-to-one. Other skills can be taught in small or medium-sized groups. Where the numbers are very small and between one and five students, this teaching methodology is often described as a tutorial. The tutorial system was, and still remains, strongly associated with Oxford and Cambridge Universities and is highly resource intensive. It seeks to encourage independent critical thinking through problem-solving, argument, and effective communication.[74]

At their most intensive, tutorials themselves can be one-to-one environments between the tutor and the student and involve the preparation and presentation of weekly written essays or papers. Due to the resource intensity of the tutorial and increasing student enrolments, together with political and academic pressures, medium-sized learning environments are more common in adult learning. Often also called seminars or workshops, they involve between twelve to thirty students meeting regularly with the seminar or workshop leader over a semester or a year.

---

[74] F. Markham, *Oxford* (London: Weidenfeld and Nicolson, 1967); W. Moore W, *The Tutorial System and its Future* (Oxford: Pergamon Press, 1968); D. Palfreyman, ed., *The Oxford Tutorial.* (Oxford: OxCHEPS, 2008).

In contrast to self-directed learning, the demonstrated advantages of small group learning are that scholastic outcomes, social and interpersonal relationships and well-being can be improved.[75] From a psychological perspective,[76] the building or development of groups is vital. Tuckman's model for group development (see figure 4.1) has been highly influential.

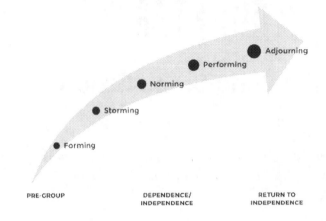

Figure 4.1. Tuckman's Five Stages of Group Development

Both the tutorial and seminar format often adopt the "Socratic method"—the tutor or seminar leader asking questions using varied techniques from argument-based, probing, or challenging to, effectively, cross-examination. In addition to each of the practical teaching techniques referred to in chapter 3, a myriad of teaching approaches that are effective in small groups (such as tutorials, seminars, and workshops) have been developed. At their core is questioning, guidance, and repetition—by the teacher and also by students individually and in groups (see figure 4.2). Each of these methodologies can utilise varying types of technologies (including AI) to enhance the teaching and learning experience (see Chapter 9).

---

[75] D. Johnson, et al., "Cooperative Learning: Improving University Instruction by Basing Practice on Validated Theory", *Journal on Excellence in College Teaching*, 25 (2014), 85.

[76] B. Tuckman, "Developmental Sequence in Small Groups", *Psychological Bulletin*, 65 (1965), 384; B. Lakey, *Facilitating Group Learning: Strategies for Success with Adult Learners* (Jossey-Bass, 2010).

Description	Approach
Brainstorm	Free flow of ideas, which are noted and then discussed.
Case study	Detailed consideration of an issue, often involving incremental learning, which can carry over more than one teaching period or seminar.
Group work	The seminar group itself is divided into groups. The groups collaborate on problem-solving for specific time periods, and then the problem and its solutions/issues are discussed by the whole seminar group.
Intensity	Intense analysis of an issue or topic followed by more reflective discussion (can be in groups of two or more and can involve the merger or "snowball" of a small group into a larger group).
Paper/project presentation	A paper or project prepared ahead of time is presented by a student (or group of students) and then discussed by the whole seminar group.
Poll	The tutor polls the class on an issue and, if there is divergence, students present differing perspectives.
Questions and answers	Questions are identified by the tutor or seminar leader and students provide answers (individually or from their groups). Often these are best also written on whiteboards or captured using classroom technology for students to be able to note themselves and as a record of the seminar's discussion.
Quizzes	Individual or group responses to a variety of set questions.
Role play / simulation	Students perform / act out roles based on factual or simulated situations and reflect on the issues.
Self-assessment	Individual tasks and exercises, which may then be brought back to the group for discussion and analysis
Warm-ups and Wind-downs	Activities at the commencement of a seminar (warm-ups) and at the end (wind-downs) can motivate increased participation in the seminar. They are an effective way to introduce new topics and to recap on the depth of understanding achieved.

Figure 4.2: Small Group Teaching Methodologies

Ultimately, the use of a variety of carefully selected techniques is highly beneficial—variety is the spice of life!

4.2 The CAISSEP Technique and Small Groups

The CAISSEP technique has specific benefits when teaching small groups. In particular, it can be used as a framework for the seminar programme and its individual seminars, but it also provides a checklist or guide to ensure the achievement of learning outcomes and the creation of an environment for "discovery" moments.

Technique	Emphasis	Style	CAISSEP for Small Groups
CAISSEP. CLARITY	Easy to comprehend teaching and learning techniques that are readily apparent; distinctive; and explanatory of their content, tasks, and assessments	Clear, open, transparent, explanatory	❖ Prepare well-prepared teaching materials ❖ Explain key concepts ❖ Identify linkages between content, tasks, and assessment ❖ Identify timing and nature of tasks and assessments ❖ Be clear about the technologies (including AI) to be used by, and in, small groups
CAISSEP. ANALYSIS	Active analytical investigation of problems, issues, and trends	Active, argument-based, experiential, solution-based and offering critical analysis, issue identification, advice, and judgement.	❖ Encourage participation ❖ Encourage inquiry ❖ Encourage discussion ❖ Encourage collaboration and group work ❖ Encourage the use of analytical technologies (including AI)

Technique	Emphasis	Style	CAISSEP for Small Groups
CAISSEP. INQUIRY	Relevant, inquisitive questioning based on self-directed learning and discovery	Autonomous, inquiring, eager for knowledge, involved	❖ **Use open questioning** ❖ **Provide problem-based tasks** ❖ **Encourage self-directed learning** ❖ **Encourage role play and simulation** ❖ **Vary the inquiry method from short "burst" to detailed consideration** ❖ **Encourage critical analysis of results derived from the use of technologies (including AI)**
CAISSEP. SYSTEM	Orderly provision of information and data that is based on principles, categories, and precedent	In-depth, detailed, informative, astute, discriminating	❖ **Identify "where things fit"** ❖ **Identify relationships between topics, weeks, and subjects** ❖ **Utilise technologies (including AI) to order, review and categorise information**
CAISSEP. STRUCTURE	Relevant, balanced, and logical consideration of issues by the use of consistent organised frameworks and methodical approaches	Reflective, analytical, organised, planned	❖ **Provide learning materials well in advance** ❖ **Draw on prior learning** ❖ **Structure teaching logically and consistently** ❖ **Use lesson planning** ❖ **Identify when, and how, technologies (including AI) will be used by, and in, small groups**

Technique	Emphasis	Style	CAISSEP for Small Groups
C A I S S E P . **EMPHASIS**	Emphatic, critical, focused, challenging, impactful	Clear highlighting of foundational issues, concepts, and principles	❖ **Introduce a preliminary overview of key concepts** ❖ **Provide "recap" mini-lectures of issues / lessons learnt** ❖ **Utilise technologies (including AI) to summarise and highlight key concepts**
C A I S S E P . **PROFESSIONAL**	Emphasis on professional and ethical considerations integrated with reflective awareness	Professional, ethical, considered, fair, just, reflective	❖ **Use a professional approach— with enthusiasm!** ❖ **Create opportunities to reflect on learning, materials, and outstanding issues** ❖ **Receive, review, and act on feedback** ❖ **Ensure a safe and respectful environment** ❖ **Reflect on the use of technologies (including AI) and their impact or influence on the outcomes and dynamics of the small groups**

Figure 4.3: The CAISSEP technique and small groups

4.3. Inviting Participation

Some of the above teaching techniques are student-led and others are teacher-driven. Where they require active guidance and input by the teacher, they call for participation by students in the class. Whilst often challenging to students, particularly new students, questions invite and motivate participation. Participation involves:

1. Planning—knowing your audience and preparing your questions ahead of time.
2. Varying your technique—the techniques should suit the learning outcomes and the time permitted.

3. Setting expectations—make it clear that seminars will involve participation.
4. Framing questions appropriately and using a variety of question-framing techniques such as:[77]
   a. *fact-finding questions*—"What kind of information do you need for this topic?"
   b. *feeling-finding questions*—"How do you feel about this topic?"
   c. *tell-me-more questions*—"Can you give specific examples that relate to this topic?"
   d. *best/least questions*—"Can you identify the best/worst thing about this topic?"
   e. *third-party questions*—"This topic can be challenging to others. How do you find this topic?"
   f. *"magic-wand" questions*—"In a perfect world, how would this topic …"
   g. *devil's advocate questions*—"We are tending towards option B. Doesn't it have similar weaknesses to option A?
   h. *confirmation questions*—"Is it right that this topic …?"
   i. *restatement questions*—"Based on our discussion, my understanding of the topic is …"
   j. *catch-all questions*—"Is there anything else about this topic we should be considering?"
   k. *permission questions*—"Is it okay if I ask you about this topic?"
   l. *reconsideration questions* – "What new information would make you change your mind?"[78]
5. Permit reflection prior to taking answers—whether it be a simple pause or a statement, such as, "Please reflect on that for a few seconds."
6. Recognise, encourage, and affirm your audience—thank the person who answers for the response or, as appropriate, praise participants for their response ("good", "that's right", and so on.).

---

[77] I. Bens, *Facilitating with Ease!* (San Francisco: John Wiley and Sons Inc, Jossey-Bass, 2012); B. Karge, et al., "Effective Strategies for Engaging Adult Learners", *Journal of College Teaching and Learning*, 8 (2011), 53. Effective and culturally sensitive strategies to encourage participation and to assess student knowledge are to direct questions to the whole class (rather than one student) and to ask students to work in pairs (see techniques in Chapter 3); N. Harrison and J. Sellwood, *"Learning and Teaching in Aboriginal and Torres Strait Islander Education"* (Oxford University Press, 4th Edition, 2022), 93.

[78] Known as "Alexander's Question" it invites reconsideration of judgments and assumptions and also promotes "analytical humility" by forcing participants to consider whether their "initial judgment might, in fact, be wrong"; C Vandepeer, *Applied Thinking for Intelligence Analysis: A Guide for Practitioners*, Commonwealth of Australia, (2014), 41-42.

4.4. Group Size

The selection of group size is important from a learning and teaching perspective. The size and composition of the group needs to allow for student learning and participation, support a range of learning capabilities, and be practical and manageable. The adages "two heads are better than one" and "many hands make light work" are often true. Indeed, research supports the conclusion that larger groups generally perform better;[79] are more likely to retain information;[80] and, importantly, formulate answers that are more accurate.[81]

However, if the group is too large, then non-participation or freeloading can occur, and workloads can be distributed unequally. Large groups have also been found to present less opportunities for leadership and achieve less consensus.[82] By contrast, if the group is too small, groups can fragment, and any further reduction in numbers can create learning tensions and unfair workload requirements.

Ultimately, a group is a decision-making entity in a learning environment. Effective eye contact between group members and the opportunity for interaction to occur and for contributions to be made is vital. In the virtual classroom and with social distancing, the opportunity for actual eye contact is more limited. In universities in Australia, the preferred group size within a seminar group is four to six students.[83] This enables a sufficient critical mass of students; the beneficial allocation of workload; the opportunity for rotating leadership responsibilities; and, if an odd number is selected, circuit-breaking capacity to avoid tied decision-making.

---

[79] G. Stewart, "A Meta-Analytic Review of Relationships between Team Design Features and Team Performance", *Journal of Management*, 32 (2006), 29.

[80] I. Horowitz and K. Bordens, "The Effects of Jury Size, Evidence Complexity and Note Taking on Jury Process and Performance in a Civil Trial", *Journal of Applied Psychology* (2002), 121.

[81] R. Bray, et al., "Effects of Group Size, Problem Difficulty, and Sex on Group Performance and Member Reactions", *Journal of Personality and Social Psychology*, 36 (1978), 1,224.

[82] R. Ziller, "Group Size: A Determinant of the Quality and Stability of Group Decisions", *Sociometry*, 20 (1957), 165.

[83] S. Soboroff, "Group size and the Trust, Cohesion, and Commitment of Group Members", PhD thesis, University of Iowa, 2012.

Review of chapter 4 Having read this chapter, you will be able to:	
1	Identify how group (or subgroup) work can be used in small group teaching
2	Identify two different inquiry-based teaching techniques that can be used for small groups
3	Describe two methods that assist in providing structure in small group teaching
4	Describe three aspects of feedback in teaching small groups
5	Prepare one "feeling-finding" and one "magic-wand" question for use in a small-group seminar relating to, say, world adult literacy levels
6	Identify the strengths and weakness of selecting groups of three for a seminar

CHAPTER 5

Teaching Large Groups and Team Teaching

When the untapped potential of a student meets the liberating art of a teacher, a miracle unfolds.

—Mary Hatwood Futrell

5.1 The Pressure of Limited Resources

Teaching requires resources. The larger the number of enrolled students, the greater the pressure on teachers to have to teach larger numbers of students in larger teaching environments. The negative impact on teaching quality and learning outcomes can be considerable and includes concerns about dropout rates and implications for equity and efficiency.[84] It can also lead to a casualisation of staffing arrangements.[85] These pressures can come from teaching organisations themselves and from government policies.

In the late twentieth century, it was said that the mass class offered "special problems that the normal class does not, and perhaps special opportunities as well, but also demands special procedures and preparation".[86] Initiated by the University of Manitoba in 2008, the MOOC (Massive Open Online Course) allows for open large number enrolments and has been adopted for a variety of courses worldwide.

---

[84] OECD, *Assessment of Higher Education Learning Outcomes, Feasibility Study Report—Design and Implementation* 1 (2012), 30–31.

[85] H. Coates, et al., "Australia's Casual Approach to its Academic Teaching Workforce", *People and Place*, 17 (2009), 47; J. Berry, *Reclaiming the Ivory Tower: Organizing Adjuncts to Save Higher Education* (Monthly Review Press, 2005).

[86] R. McGee, *Teaching the Mass Class* (2nd edn, Washington, American Sociological Association 1991), vi.

5.2. Team Teaching: Leadership

The management of large groups requires leadership. Teaching large groups requires leadership, collaboration, and mutual support. Many different methodologies are adopted for the team teaching of large groups. Figure 5.1. describes the most common in universities.[87]

Type	Methodology
"General"	Topic coordinator acts as a general and assigns teaching, marking, and other tasks to other members of the team
Collaboration	All members of the teaching team work together, often with one as a "leader" for reporting purposes
Parallel teaching	Different teachers take responsibility for different students within a subject and teach them in parallel
Split teaching	Different teachers take responsibility for different subjects or topics within the programme and teach and mark those selected subjects

Figure 5.1. Teaching Large Group Methodologies

5.3. The Lecture/Seminar Combination: What Is Its Appeal?

The delivery of information in adult education environments has commonly relied upon the lecture, now often recorded for student access. The "flipped" classroom has been discussed in chapter 3, and the seminar has been discussed in chapter 4. Each of these techniques integrates together in the teaching of large groups and very often in combination with the lecture format.

Why a lecture? Drawing on history and the science of learning and teaching, there are a few reasons. The lecture is a relatively easy way to inform many, in one place, and at low cost. In addition, the lecture provides an opportunity for communication to occur, predominantly by the lecturer, which is both auditory and visual. In many situations, students are able to ask questions, there and then, which enable their own queries to be answered and can often also reflect the queries of others. The lecture can provide information, motivation, direction, and context efficiently and clearly. The lecture permits the lecturer to control the content, pace, and delivery of the lecture materials.

By contrast, lectures often are passive from the student's perspective; provide little opportunity

---

[87] S. Kift, et al., *Excellence and Innovation in Legal Education* (Lexis Nexis Butterworths, 2011), 174.

to gauge the extent of student learning; rely upon effective communication; and are not ideal for advanced analysis, evaluation, or reflection by students.

5.4. The Use of Entertainment and Humour

Grabbing and retaining the attention of students is a challenge. Students have many distractions, both inside and outside the classroom. The use of technology in the classroom enables the technology itself, with all its social media diversions, to be employed by students. The classroom needs to reflect society or, in the case of clinical practice teaching (see chapter 6), the workplace. In order to do so, a contemporary, information-rich, technology-filled environment is more compatible with students' life experience than a sterile, laboratory-like domain. Accordingly, a hybrid form of education has arisen, which seeks to replicate popular entertainment in the classroom and lecture hall—sometimes known as "edutainment".

Humour does not require technology. Dry deadpan humour can involve no expression and still entertain and be funny. Humour is a natural human gift, and it should be used in teaching. It can reduce stress and anxiety, improve information retention, increase subject enjoyment, enhance teacher-student relationships, and promote student engagement.[88] In fact, as one researcher put it:

> It could be convincingly argued that what counts as a "good teacher" within the contemporary university sector has little in common with the same "good teacher" from 100 years ago. We are now firmly in the pedagogic era of edutainment, wherein students have come to expect a particular kind of performance from their lecturers and tutors, particularly those who wish to be regarded as good at what they do.[89]

When employing humour in teaching, as with humour itself, there are a number of key elements—content, communication, originality, timing, and context. In a teaching environment, these will require reflection and care, particularly content and context. Adopting the CAISSEP technique, humour can emphasise topics, highlight real-world inconsistencies, enhance learning, and nurture moments of happiness. Whenever it is employed in the classroom, humour should always be culturally sensitive, inclusive, and non-discriminatory (see chapter 7).

---

[88] G. Tait, et al., "Laughing with the Lecturer: The Use of Humour in Shaping University Teaching, *Journal of University Teaching & Learning Practice* (2015), 1–2.

[89] Tait, et al., "Laughing with the Lecturer", 13.

5.5 The CAISSEP Technique and Large Groups

Technique	Emphasis	Style	CAISSEP for Large Groups
CAISSEP. CLARITY	Easy to comprehend teaching and learning techniques that are readily apparent; distinctive; and explanatory of their content, tasks and assessments.	Clear, open, transparent, explanatory	❖ **Coordinate a well-defined team** ❖ **Allocate roles clearly and consistently** ❖ **Use well-prepared teaching materials** ❖ **Provide explanations of key concepts** ❖ **Identify linkages between content, tasks, and assessment** ❖ **Identify timing and nature of tasks and assessments** ❖ **Be clear about the technologies (including AI) to be used by, and in, large groups**
CAISSEP. ANALYSIS	Active, analytical investigation of problems, issues and trends.	Active, argument-based, experiential, solution-based and offering critical analysis, issue identification, advice, and judgement.	❖ **Ensure consistency across problems and issues** ❖ **Provide "standard" teaching and problem materials but allow individual flexibility** ❖ **Identify opportunities for participation, inquiry, and discussion** ❖ **Encourage the use of analytical technologies (including AI)**

Technique	Emphasis	Style	CAISSEP for Large Groups
CAISSEP. **INQUIRY**	Relevant, inquisitive questioning based on self-directed learning and discovery	Autonomous, inquiring, eager for knowledge, involved	❖ **Create questioning opportunities** ❖ **Encourage self-directed learning** ❖ **Involve students in their own learning** ❖ **Encourage critical analysis of results derived from the use of technologies (including AI)**
CAISSEP. **SYSTEM**	Orderly provision of information and data that is based on principles, categories, and precedent	In-depth, detailed, informative, astute, discriminating	❖ **Identify "where things fit"** ❖ **Identify relationships between topics, weeks, and subjects** ❖ **Utilise technologies (including AI) to order, review and categorise information**

Technique	Emphasis	Style	CAISSEP for Large Groups
CAISSEP. STRUCTURE	Relevant, balanced, logical consideration of issues by the use of consistent organised frameworks and methodical approaches	Reflective, analytical, organised, planned	❖ **Provide learning materials well in advance** ❖ **Draw on prior learning** ❖ **Structure teaching logically and consistently** ❖ **Adopt a clear format— beginning (what you are going to say), middle (what you want to say), and end (what has been said)** ❖ **Use lesson planning** ❖ **Identify what students will have learnt and be able to do at the end of the lecture** ❖ **Identify when, and how, technologies (including AI) will be used by, and in, large groups**
CAISSEP. EMPHASIS	Emphatic, focused challenging, impactful	Clear highlighting of foundational issues, concepts and principles	❖ **Introduce preliminary overviews of key concepts** ❖ **Provide "recap" mini-lectures of issues/lessons learnt** ❖ **Engage students with the materials** ❖ **Utilise technologies (including AI) to summarise and highlight key concepts**

Technique	Emphasis	Style	CAISSEP for Large Groups
CAISSEP. PROFESSIONAL	Emphasis on professional and ethical considerations integrated with reflective awareness	Professional, ethical, considered, fair, just, reflective	❖ **Professional approach—with enthusiasm!** ❖ **Create opportunities to reflect on learning, materials and outstanding issues** ❖ **Use humour (carefully)** ❖ **Receive, review, and act on feedback** ❖ **Ensure a safe and respectful environment** ❖ **Reflect on the use of technologies (including AI) and their impact or influence on the outcome and dynamics of the large group**

Figure 5.2. CAISSEP technique and Large Group

5.6. Teach the Teacher or "Train the Trainer"

Another role of the lead teacher is often to train others. There are various forms in which this occurs, and various expressions have been adopted; "teaching the teacher" or "training the trainer" are the most common. The nature of the role will vary depending upon, broadly, three scenarios—the experience of the teacher to be trained, whether new skills are to be learned, or whether feedback on new programmes is being sought.

Where the teacher to be trained requires improvement, the lead teacher acts as an expert and teaches or facilitates new techniques or materials. Where new skills are to be learned, the lead teacher leads the instruction and assists with skill development. Where new programmes are proposed or variations to delivery modes are being considered, the lead teacher acts as a demonstrator, and feedback is received from the participants.

Review of chapter 5	
Having read this chapter, you will be able to:	
1	Identify two methods of managing the teaching of large groups
2	Describe two CAISSEP teaching techniques to enhance clarity when teaching large groups
3	Describe how professionalism enhances teaching outcomes in large groups
4	Identify two different scenarios that may require "teach the teacher" instruction

CHAPTER 6

Clinical Practice Teaching and Teaching Postgraduate Students

We can teach from our experience, but we cannot teach experience.

—Sasha Azevedo

6.1. The More Experienced Student

Clinical teaching involves building on existing knowledge and overlaying it with clinical awareness and experience. Whilst these teaching environments seek to replicate true clinical situations, they are often more "mock", "simulated", or "cotton-wool" replicas by nature. In Australia, a criterion for teaching is the evaluation of practice within the relevant profession or discipline and continuing professional development.[90] The closer these teaching environments are to real world practice or problems, the more effective the learning experience.

Another type of more experienced student is the postgraduate student. The postgraduate student who is undertaking a taught course[91] does not have the benefit of the close supervision and support

---

[90] Australian Government Office for Learning and Teaching, *Australian Universities Teaching Criteria*, Criteria 6.

[91] Compared to a research programme such as postgraduate doctoral degree. See B. Kamler and P. Thomson, *Helping Doctoral Students Write: Pedagogies for Supervision* (Routledge, 2006); C. Roulston, "Supervising a Doctoral Student", *Teaching Politics and International Relations* (2012)m 210; E. Phillips and D. Pugh, *How to Get a PhD: A Handbook for Students and their Supervisors* (4th edn, Maidenhead, UK: Open University Press, 2005); G. Wisker, *The Good Supervisor: Supervising Postgraduate and Undergraduate Research for Doctoral Theses and Dissertations* (New York: Palgrave Macmillan, 2005).

network of a supervisor like, say, in a doctoral research programme. However, the student who has a prior degree (or degrees) and is undertaking either a clinical practice programme or a postgraduate degree does have a number of characteristics in common with the doctoral research student:

1. prior experience with the discipline
2. an enthusiasm for the discipline
3. an intention to apply prior learning in a practical or theoretical environment upon completion of the course
4. a thirst for knowledge and for the prior experience and knowledge of the teacher to be shared
5. an expectation that there will be professionalism, feedback (positive in nature and also constructive criticism), and timeliness in the teaching relationship and the course
6. a recognition that the course will present challenges and that life's events will require flexibility, understanding, and support
7. a capacity for, and the nurturing of an environment that promotes, independent and autonomous learning to enable the student to further his or her development.

Each of these factors requires the teacher and student to interact efficiently and professionally. The opportunity for a teacher to teach a motivated student and for a student to learn from an experienced encouraging teacher is the heart of teaching. However, clinical practice also has a higher purpose—service:

> Professional education is preparation for accomplished and responsible practice in the service of others … Thus the pedagogies of the professions must attempt to bridge and resolve tensions between the competing imperatives to which future professionals must respond. The students must learn abundant amounts of theory and vast bodies of knowledge, but the "bottom line" of their efforts will not be what they know but what they can do.[92]

6.2. The Life Cycle of the Diverse or International Student

Students travel the globe to undertake international studies. Universities compete to attract international or diverse students to their campuses and to undertake online programmes. As a result, university communities, campuses, and curricula become more diverse and interesting and linkages

---

[92] Sullivan, et al., *Educating Lawyers*, 23.

that can be lifelong are created. With the advent of the coronavirus pandemic, the flow of students internationally has been interrupted and, in many places, stalled.

To forge, improve, and maintain teaching and learning relationships for the international student, a "life cycle" approach is required. This approach differs from the considerations applicable to the domestic student. Each step of the way, the cultural diversity of the student is relevant to the approach to be taken (see figure 6.1., as well as chapter 7).

Figure 6.1. International Student Teaching "Life Cycle"

6.3. Mentoring

Teaching is often described, interchangeably, as a form of mentoring.[93] Mentors guide mentees with advice, support, and assistance and share their own experience, often also assisting with career progression. Mentors can be within, or external to, an organisation. The mentor/mentee relationship is often semi-structured or even informal.

At the turn of the century, it was forecast, accurately, that mentoring was moving in four directions:

---

[93] J. Barnett, et al. "Clinical Supervision, Teaching, and Mentoring", *The Clinical Supervisor*, 20 (2002), 217.

1. moving from pairs (mentor/mentee) to being more integrated in the organisational culture
2. moving away from classroom work only to developing broader relationships
3. devolving from the hierarchical delivery of experience to undertaking shared inquiries in professional practice
4. moving away from isolation from the teaching system itself to being more integrated within, and improving, the teaching system.[94]

Mentoring programmes are now commonplace across diverse teaching environments, workplaces, and organisations. It is vital that they are developed conscientiously and within a suitable framework.[95] An example of a mentoring framework from induction to professional identity is shown in figure 6.2.

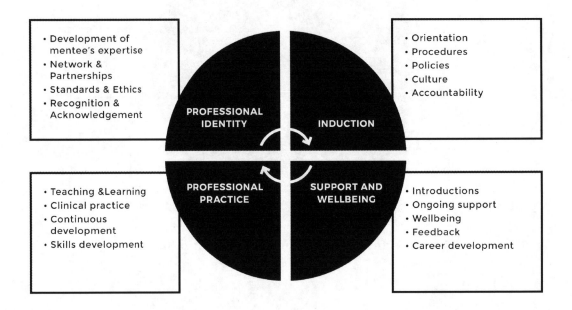

Figure 6.2. Mentoring Framework

Mentoring requires a dedicated team, clear goals, and highly effective communication. The mentoring that is provided must be relevant, and the mentors must have the necessary experience. Mentors, often more than one, need to be suitable and trained effectively. Mentees need to be

---

[94] A. Hargreaves and M. Fullan, "Mentoring in the New Millennium", *Theory into Practice* (2000), 50, 56.

[95] S. Welsch, *Mentoring the Future: A Guide to Building Mentor Programs that Work* (Global Book, 2004).

identified and then matched with mentors. Preferably, mentees should have some say in the choice of their mentor, as, in doing so, they are more invested in the relationship.[96] There also needs to be a capacity for confidential and open feedback and for necessary adjustment, refinement, or change. Genuine feedback opportunities about the programme itself also need to be provided, and there must be some measurement of the programme's quality and outcomes through review, preferably by independent reviews.

6.4. The CAISSEP Technique and Clinical Practice Teaching and Teaching Postgraduate Students

Technique	Emphasis	Style	CAISSEP˙ for Clinical Practice & Postgraduate Students
CAISSEP. CLARITY	Easy to comprehend teaching and learning techniques that are readily apparent; distinctive; and explanatory of their content, tasks, and assessments	Clear, open, transparent, explanatory	❖ **Coordinate a well-defined team** ❖ **Allocate roles clearly and consistently** ❖ **Use well-prepared practice or postgraduate teaching materials** ❖ **Provide explanations of key concepts** ❖ **Identify linkages between content, tasks, and assessment** ❖ **Identify timing and nature of tasks and assessments** ❖ **Be clear about the technologies (including AI) to be used in clinical practice and postgraduate students**

---

[96] D. Clutterbuck, et al., *Mentoring and Diversity: An International Perspective* (Oxford, 2002).

Technique	Emphasis	Style	CAISSEP® for Clinical Practice & Postgraduate Students
CAISSEP. ANALYSIS	Active analytical investigation of problems, issues, and trends	Active, argument-based, experiential, solution-based and offering critical analysis, issue identification, advice, and judgement.	❖ **Ensure consistency across problems and issues** ❖ **Provide "standard" teaching and problem materials but allow individual flexibility** ❖ **Identify opportunities for participation, inquiry, and discussion** ❖ **Support practice and postgraduate students by your presence, time, and attentive listening** ❖ **Encourage the use of analytical technologies (including AI)**
CAISSEP. INQUIRY	Relevant inquisitive questioning based on self-directed learning and discovery	Autonomous, inquiring, eager for knowledge, involved	❖ **Create questioning opportunities** ❖ **Encourage self-directed learning** ❖ **Involve practice or postgraduate students in their own learning** ❖ **Use questions to encourage practice or postgraduate students to identify their own needs, motivations, and ambitions** ❖ **Encourage critical analysis of results derived from the use of technologies (including AI)**

Technique	Emphasis	Style	CAISSEP' for Clinical Practice & Postgraduate Students
CAISSEP. SYSTEM	Orderly provision of information and data that is based on principles, categories, and precedent	In-depth, detailed, informative, astute, discriminating	❖ **Identify "where things fit"** ❖ **Identify relationships between topics, weeks, and subjects** ❖ **Utilise technologies (including AI) to order, review and categorise information**
CAISSEP. STRUCTURE	Relevant, balanced, and logical consideration of issues by the use of consistent organised frameworks and methodical approaches	Reflective, analytical, organised, planned	❖ **Provide practice or postgraduate learning materials well in advance** ❖ **Draw on prior learning** ❖ **Structure practice or postgraduate teaching logically and consistently** ❖ **Adopt a clear format— beginning (what you are going to say), middle (what you want to say), and end (what has been said)** ❖ **Use lesson planning** ❖ **Identify what practice and postgraduate students will have learnt and be able to do at the end of the session or programme** ❖ **Identify when, and how, technologies (including AI) will be used by clinical practice and postgraduate students**

Technique	Emphasis	Style	CAISSEP° for Clinical Practice & Postgraduate Students
CAISSEP. EMPHASIS	Emphatic, focused, challenging, impactful	Clear highlighting of foundational issues, concepts and principles	❖ **Introduce preliminary overviews of key concepts** ❖ **Provide "recap" mini-lectures of issues / lessons learnt** ❖ **Engage practice and postgraduate students with the materials** ❖ **Utilise technologies (including AI) to summarise and highlight key concepts**
CAISSEP. PROFESSIONAL	Emphasis on professional and ethical considerations integrated with reflective awareness	Professional, ethical, considered, fair, just, reflective	❖ **Professional approach—with enthusiasm!** ❖ **Create opportunities to reflect on practice and postgraduate learning, materials, and outstanding issues** ❖ **Use humour (carefully)** ❖ **Receive, review, and act on feedback** ❖ **Ensure safe, caring, and respectful practice and postgraduate teaching environments** ❖ **Encourage practice and professional students to act professionally and to develop professional forward-looking ethical perspectives**

Technique	Emphasis	Style	CAISSEP˙ for Clinical Practice & Postgraduate Students
			❖ **Reflect on the use of technologies (including AI) and their impact or influence on the outcomes and dynamics of clinical practice and postgraduate teaching environments**

Figure 6.3. Clinical Practice Teaching and Teaching Postgraduate methodologies

Review of chapter 6 **Having read this chapter, you will be able to:**	
1	Identify three characteristics of the postgraduate student that provide teaching and learning opportunities
2	Identify how cultural diversity involves a "life cycle" for an international student
3	Identify the four elements of a mentoring framework
4	Describe why the use of the CAISSEP technique and its emphasis on structure is important to an international or postgraduate student

CHAPTER 7

Culturally Sensitive and Inclusive Teaching

When curriculum is standardized to state policies and does not consider the native language, traditions and customs of the people, this creates a barrier that most indigenous people are unable to overcome.[97]

—Natalee, teacher, Bay Islands, Honduras

Culture is communication and communication is culture. People cannot act or interact at all in any meaningful way except through the medium of culture.

—Edward Hall

7.1. Culturally Sensitive and Inclusive Teaching: Building Understanding and Trust

When we teach, we present ourselves to an audience and seek to build a community. It's important that the teaching environment makes no assumptions and that it accommodates differences through culturally sensitive and inclusive teaching. The primary challenge is to focus on how students learn and to establish a supportive learning environment. This enables us to encourage students to develop their learning behaviours positively and promotes inclusion and collaboration. Culture includes a student's gender, race, religion or beliefs, age, disability, and ethnicity.

The real world is highly diverse. Real-world learning draws upon real-world contexts and enables students to explore their own identities, independence, beliefs, aspirations, and global citizenship.

At the core of the teacher-student relationship is communication, access, understanding and

---

[97] UNESCO, *Teaching and Learning*, 287.

trust. Understanding is an active process and requires both intellectual and emotional sensitivity. Trust is not to be assumed.

Methods to achieve understanding and trust include:

1. information sessions,
2. welcome occasions,
3. introductions by students in seminars of themselves and their cultures,
4. establishing and maintaining dialogue,
5. taking positive steps to understand the student's cultures and identities,
6. the maintenance of confidentiality,
7. clarity about what your role is and what you can and cannot assist with based on your role and the organisation's function, and
8. an awareness that trust is earned and an environment of trust may take time to build.

7.2. Building Cultural Competence

Often cultural diversity and inclusion issues have implications on the students' capacity to participate fully in society, as well as their learning experience. These can be improved by teachers:

1. undertaking cross-cultural and anti-discrimination training;
2. ensuring that materials, presentations, and communication methods are non-discriminatory, inclusive, and culturally sensitive;
3. critically reflecting on institutional, professional, and own cultures to appreciate their limitations; and
4. committing to cultural change and increasing cultural understanding and diversity.

The development of cultural competency, in the context of indigenous Australians, in universities has identified five guiding principles.[98] These principles, which can be applied equally to all adult education institutions, are:

❖ active involvement by indigenous Australians in governance and management
❖ ensuring cultural competence of Australian graduates

---

[98] Universities Australia, *National Best Practice Framework for Indigenous Cultural Competency in Australian Universities* (Canberra: Department of Education, Employment and Workplace Relations, 2011).; see also N. Harrison and J. Sellwood, *"Learning and Teaching in Aboriginal and Torres Strait Islander Education"* (Oxford University Press, 4th Edition, 2022).

❖ including culturally competent research that empowers indigenous participants and encourages collaborations with indigenous communities

❖ increasing indigenous staffing at all appointment levels and, for academic staff, across a wider variety of academic fields

❖ forming operational partnerships with indigenous communities and facilitating the dissemination of culturally competent practices to the wider community.

A development model of cultural competence that provides a guide for the development of strategies for culturally competent engagement in professional practice has been identified[99] and is presented in figure 7.1.

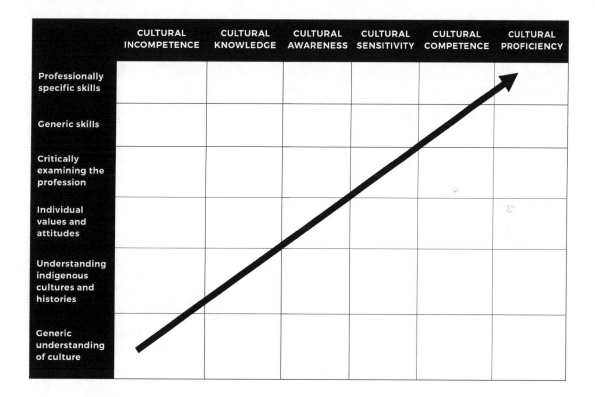

Figure 7.1. Development Model for Cultural Competence

---

[99] R. Ranzijn, et al., "Introduction to Cultural Competence", in *Psychology and Indigenous Australians: Foundations of Cultural Competence* (Palgrave/ Macmillan, 2009), 10.

7.3. Disability Action Plans and Special Needs

In most adult learning institutions, formal disability action plans (DAPs) are prepared at the start of the academic year in collaboration with the student by learning specialists and often health specialists with specialised skills. These plans seek to provide support for students with a diverse range of disabilities such as medical and mental health conditions, learning difficulties, or disabilities that impact study. DAPs are provided to teaching staff on a confidential basis, and advice is provided and agreed upon as to necessary adjustments and accommodation for individual student learning.

Students who require flexibility to their study and the tailoring of their learning programme can be subjects of specialist schemes. For example, an elite athlete may require flexibility whilst training or competing at an elite level in his or her chosen sport.[100] In Australia, the Elite Athletes Admissions Scheme provides a pathway for elite sportspeople to facilitate their university studies.

7.4. The CAISSEP Technique and Culturally Sensitive and Inclusive Teaching

Technique	Emphasis	Style	CAISSEP for Culturally Sensitive and Inclusive Teaching
CAISSEP. CLARITY	Easy to comprehend teaching and learning techniques that are readily apparent; distinctive; and explanatory of their content, tasks, and assessments	Clear, open, transparent, explanatory	❖ Prepare culturally aware and inclusive teaching materials ❖ Ensure timing and nature of tasks and assessments is culturally aware and inclusive ❖ Ensure technology (including AI) is culturally aware and inclusive

---

[100] J. Cheville, *Minding the Body: What Student Athletes Know about Learning* (Heinemann USA, 2001).

Technique	Emphasis	Style	CAISSEP for Culturally Sensitive and Inclusive Teaching
CAISSEP. **ANALYSIS**	Active analytical investigation of problems, issues, and trends	Active, argument-based, experiential, solution-based and offering critical analysis, issue identification, advice, and judgement.	❖ **Identify opportunities for participation, inquiry, and discussion based on culturally aware and inclusive environments and technologies (including AI)**
CAISSEP. **INQUIRY**	Relevant, inquisitive questioning based on self-directed learning and discovery	Autonomous, inquiring, eager for knowledge, involved	❖ **Involve students in their own learning based on cultural awareness and inclusivity and culturally aware and sensitive technologies (including AI)**
CAISSEP. **SYSTEM**	Orderly provision of information and data that is based on principles, categories, and precedent	In-depth, detailed, informative, astute, discriminating	❖ **Identify culturally aware and inclusive systems and practices** ❖ **Select culturally aware and inclusive technologies (including AI)**

Technique	Emphasis	Style	CAISSEP for Culturally Sensitive and Inclusive Teaching
CAISSEP. **STRUCTURE**	Relevant, balanced, and logical consideration of issues by the use of consistent organised frameworks and methodical approaches	Reflective, analytical, organised, planned	❖ **Provide culturally aware and inclusive learning materials well in advance** ❖ **Structure teaching in a culturally aware and inclusive manner** ❖ **Ensure cultural awareness and inclusiveness are part of lesson planning and the selection and adoption of technologies (including AI)**
CAISSEP. **EMPHASIS**	Emphasis, critical, focus, challenging, impactful	Clear highlighting of foundational issues, concepts and principles	❖ **Emphasise culturally aware and inclusive concepts and participation and in the selection and adoption of technologies (including AI)**

Technique	Emphasis	Style	CAISSEP for Culturally Sensitive and Inclusive Teaching
CAISSEP. PROFESSIONAL	Emphasis on professional and ethical considerations integrated with reflective awareness	Professional, ethical, considered, fair, just, reflective	❖ **Professional approach—with enthusiasm, cultural awareness, and inclusiveness!** ❖ **Create culturally aware, inclusive opportunities to reflect on learning** ❖ **Ensure safe, respectful, culturally aware, and inclusive teaching environments and in the selection and adoption of technologies (including AI)**

Figure 7.2. Culturally sensitive and inclusive teaching

	Review of chapter 7 Having read this chapter, you will be able to:
1	Identify three methods to achieve understanding and trust in the teaching environment
2	Identify three activities teachers can undertake to improve teaching and learning environments and their cultural diversity and inclusiveness
3	Describe why two aspects of professionalism in the CAISSEP technique are important to cultural diversity and inclusiveness

CHAPTER 8

The Teaching-Research Nexus

8.1. Teaching and Scholarship

Historically, academic institutions drew a functional distinction between teaching and research but with research providing vitality and impacting upon teaching.[101] In Australia, the integration of research into the teaching discipline is a required teaching criterion.[102] Influenced by Boyer,[103] research scholarship has been encouraged to divide itself into four broad categories:

- scholarship of discovery (e.g. basic research)
- scholarship of integration (for example, interdisciplinary or multidisciplinary research or "within the discipline" research)
- scholarship of application (sometimes called engagement)—within or outside the institution
- scholarship of teaching and learning (in other words, the study of teaching and learning itself).

There is an international trend to split "teaching" and "research" into subspecialties or subcategories—so much so that teaching specialists or teaching professionals often only, or principally, teach but also do research into the scholarship of teaching within their discipline. Within teaching,

---

[101] J. Perkins, "Organization and Functions of the University", *The Journal of Higher Education*, 43/9 (1972), 679, 683; G. Cutten, "The College Professor as Teacher", *School and Society*, 86 (1958), 372.

[102] Australian Government Office for Learning and Teaching, *Australian Universities Teaching Criteria*, Criteria 5.

[103] E. Boyer, *Scholarship Reconsidered: Priorities of the Professoriate* (The Carnegie Foundation for the Advancement of Teaching, 1990).

"scholarship about teaching" has itself become a specialty. Five approaches to the scholarship of teaching have been identified:[104]

    a.   improving knowledge by collecting and reading teaching literature,

    b.   improving teaching by collecting and reading teaching literature,

    c.   improving student learning by investigating the learning of one's own students and one's own teaching,

    d.   improving one's own students' learning by knowing and relating the literature on teaching and learning to discipline-specific literature and knowledge, and

    e.   improving student learning within the discipline generally by collecting and communicating results of one's own work on teaching and learning within the discipline.

For the teaching professional, there are three teaching scholarship domains:

    a.   practice of teaching,

    b.   scholarship of teaching, and

    c.   communication of teaching expertise

They are interrelated and, in combination, define the teaching professional's role and function as shown in figure 8.1.

---

[104] K. Trigwell, et al., "Scholarship of Teaching: A Model", *Higher Education Research and Development* 19/2 (2000), 55, 159.

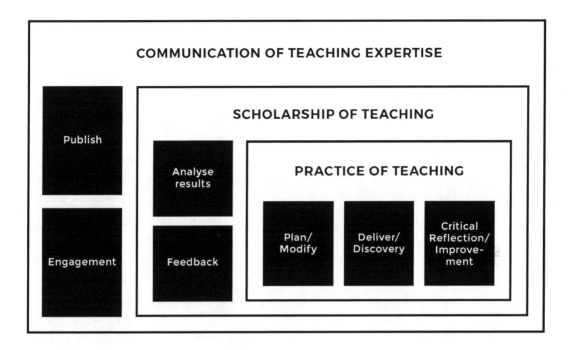

Figure 8.1. Teaching Scholarship Domains

It has been said, pragmatically, that:

> In the end, it is up to the institutions and the academics to take deliberate steps
> to create a positive nexus between teaching and research. In the ongoing academic
> conversation about the teaching-research nexus, the focus should no longer be upon
> whether a positive nexus exists between these two activities. The new focus should
> be upon how a positive nexus between teaching and research can be implemented
> and enhanced.[105]

The CAISSEP technique seeks to identify how such a positive nexus can be implemented and
enhanced.

---

[105] N. Nehme, "The Nexus between Teaching and Research: Easier Said Than Done", *Legal Education Review*,
22/2 (2012), 241.

8.2. The CAISSEP Technique and Teaching Research

Technique	Emphasis	Style	CAISSEP* for Teaching Research
C A I S S E P. **CLARITY**	Easy to comprehend teaching and learning techniques that are readily apparent; distinctive; and explanatory of their content, tasks, and assessments	Clear, open, transparent, explanatory	❖ **Allocate teaching-research roles clearly and consistently** ❖ **Ensure clear and consistent use of technology (including AI)**
C A I S S E P. **ANALYSIS**	Active analytical investigation of problems, issues, and trends	Active, argument-based, experiential, solution-based and offering critical analysis, issue identification, advice, and judgement.	❖ **Ensure consistency across teaching-research analysis** ❖ **Design learning and discovery activities to include leading research (including based on technology and AI)**
C A I S S E P. **INQUIRY**	Relevant inquisitive questioning based on self-directed learning and discovery	Autonomous, inquiring, eager for knowledge, involved	❖ **Draw on student-based learning for teaching-research** ❖ **Draw on own research in the design of courses and materials** ❖ **Teach research skills (including technology-based and involving AI) and methodologies within taught courses**

Technique	Emphasis	Style	CAISSEP* for Teaching Research
C A I S S E P ○ **S Y S T E M**	Orderly provision of information and data based on principles, categories, and precedent	In-depth, detailed, informative, astute, discriminating	❖ **Identify relationships between teaching and research** ❖ **Include the most recent research (including technology and AI-related) in teaching materials**
C A I S S E P ○ **S T R U C T U R E**	Relevant, balanced, and logical consideration of issues by the use of consistent organised frameworks and methodical approaches.	Reflective, analytical, organised, planned	❖ **Structure teaching-research logically and consistently** ❖ **Use research plans** ❖ **Structure technology (including AI) in teaching-research**
C A I S S E P ○ **E M P H A S I S**	Emphatic, focused, challenging, impactful	Clear highlighting of foundational issues, concepts and principles	❖ **Emphasise the value of teaching-research scholarship** ❖ **Emphasise the role and impact of technologies (including AI) on teaching-research scholarship**

Technique	Emphasis	Style	CAISSEP˙ for Teaching Research
    C A I S S E P . **PROFESSIONAL**	Emphasis on professional and ethical considerations integrated with reflective awareness	Professional, ethical, considered, fair, just, reflective	❖ **Professional approach to teaching-research** ❖ **Involve and mentor students in research opportunities** ❖ **Adopt an ethical, "research"-led approach to learning** ❖ **Contribute to teaching beyond your discipline** ❖ **Engage with the community** ❖ **Consider and adopt technologies (including AI) which evidence professionalism in teaching-research**

Figure 8.2. Teaching and Research methodologies

Review of chapter 8 Having read this chapter, you will be able to:	
1	Identify the four different types of research scholarship
2	Identify two approaches to the scholarship of teaching
3	Describe two ways in which professionalism plays a role in the CAISSEP technique to enhance the teaching-research nexus
4	Describe the three domains for teaching scholarship

CHAPTER 9

Teaching and Technology

*Technology is a medium that, without a doubt, facilitates learning in school,
but that will never take the place of the work of a teacher.*[106]

—Carlos, teacher, Santiago, Chile

9.1. The Technological Teaching Ecosystem

The modern adult education classroom is unrecognisable from its nineteenth- and twentieth-century forebears. In most countries and in their adult education environments, technology is commonplace. Often, there is no physical teacher "in" the classroom. Students can "attend" as virtual icons on a screen . Materials rest in remote data files. Assignments are stored in the cloud, reviewed by the application of algorithms, and marked and graded by standardised digital criteria. It is no longer a question of teaching with technology[107] or even incorporating[108] technology in teaching. The classroom, whether real or virtual, now involves an integrated, fragile environment or ecosystem

---

[106] UNESCO, *Teaching and Learning*, 291.

[107] R. Burris, et al. *Teaching Law with Computers: A Collection of Essays* (Routledge 1979); R. Lasso, "From the Paper Chase to the Digital Chase: Technology and the Challenge of Teaching 21st Century Law Students", *Santa Clara Law Review*, 43 ((2002–2003), 1; R. Sherwin, et al., "Law in the Digital Age: How Visual Communication Technologies are Transforming the Practice, Theory, and Teaching of Law", *B.U. J. Sci. & Tech. L.*, 12 (2006), 227; R. Warner, et al., "Teaching Law with Computers", *Rutgers Computer & Tech. L.J.*, 24 (1998), 107.

[108] D. Thomson D. *Law School 2.0: Legal Education for a Digital Age* (Lexis Nexis, 2009).

of teaching and technology. The United Nations has observed that the coronavirus pandemic has displaced and broken this ecosystem, and it will need to be rebuilt, or reimagined, urgently.

Each teaching environment will have different levels of technological support for the teacher and student, from the technology in the classroom itself (such as computers, projection, or recording technology) to platforms for the delivery and distribution of materials, assignments, and assessment marking. Whilst often varying across disciplines (i.e. from laboratories to mock courtrooms), institutional teaching environments adopt relatively standardised technology formats which are based upon the significant enterprise investments made by the organisation.[109]

9.2. Student-Centric Teaching Ecosystem

From a student perspective, the teaching ecosystem comprises a number of components. They will differ depending upon whether the learning environment is a traditional seminar and lecture room, a physical classroom, or an online portal. Based on the principles and techniques in this book, a student-centric teaching ecosystem for adult education is shown in figure 9.1.

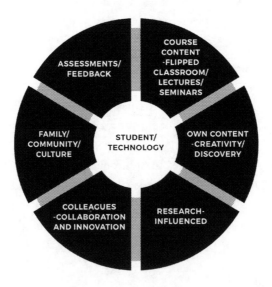

Figure 9.1. Student-Centric Teaching Ecosystem and Technology

---

[109] The "sections" technique can be used in the selection of, and investment decisions regarding, technology with its focus students, ease of use, costs, teaching functions, interaction, organisational issues, networking, and security and Privacy. A. Bates, *Teaching in a Digital Age* (Tony Bates Associates Ltd, 2015), 304.

The student-centric ecosystem also illustrates the interconnectedness of technology with the student and the learning domain.

9.3. Teaching and Artificial Intelligence (AI)

In 2023 UNESCO observed that we "have officially entered the Age of Artificial Intelligence".[110] The nature and scope of AI has evolved since it was first coined in 1956 at the Dartmouth Summer Research Project on Artificial Intelligence at Dartmouth College in New Hampshire, USA. As a result, no single definition of AI has been accepted by the international scientific community.[111] A practical, working definition of 'AI' is:[112]

> AI refers to an engineered system that generates predictive outputs such as content, forecasts, recommendations or decisions for a given set of human-defined objectives or parameters without explicit programming. AI systems are designed to operate with varying levels of automation.

The international market for education technologies, including AI, is vast and burgeoning. Hundreds of commercial applications are currently available. However, there are often gaps in available information to ensure effective, reliable decision-making by teachers and educational institutions.[113] There are many risks and, whilst privacy and data security implications are paramount, there are many others, including:[114]

---

[110] UNESCO, *Readiness Assessment Methodology – A Tool of the Recommendation on the Ethics of Artificial Intelligence*, (2023), 5.

[111] European Parliament, *Artificial intelligence act, Briefing*, (June 2023), 3.

[112] Commonwealth of Australia, *Safe and responsible AI in Australia consultation, Australian Government's interim response*, (2024) The proposed United States' *National Artificial Intelligence Act* of 2020 defines AI as meaning "a machine-based system that can, for a given set of human-defined objectives, make predictions, recommendations or decisions influencing real or virtual environments." The European Union proposed definition of an AI system is 'software that is developed with [specific] techniques and approaches [which are listed in the Act] and can, for a given set of human-defined objectives, generate outputs such as content, predictions, recommendations, or decisions influencing the environments they interact with." (Article 3(1) and Recital 6)).

[113] L. Loble, & A. Hawcroft, (2022). *Shaping AI and Edtech to Tackle Australia's Learning Divide*. University of Technology Sydney, 84 (identified a sample inventory of 200 commercially available student-, teacher- and system-oriented applications), 84-86.

[114] Commonwealth of Australia, *Safe and responsible AI in Australia consultation*, Australian Government's interim response, (2024), 4

1. inaccuracies in inputs and outputs, including misinformation
2. biased or poor-quality data
3. discriminatory inputs and outputs
4. lack of transparency about how and when AI is used

The digital divide and levels of digital literacy (or illiteracy) mean that AI is simply not available or accessible to many. Internationally, many countries also face teacher shortages and a decline in vocational education teachers.[115] The use of AI by those who can access it has the potential to expand, rather than reduce, the digital divide to the point where "AI-empowered professionals will outpace those who don't take advantage of this era of transformation".[116] The ability to use AI assumes 'digital' literacy when literacy levels internationally are manifestly too low. Research demonstrates, powerfully, that:[117]

> only edtech that is properly designed, used and regulated can have a demonstrably positive impact on learning outcomes for disadvantaged students.

Regulatory and ethical "guardrails" are proposed to avoid AI reproducing real world biases and discrimination, fueling divisions and threatening fundamental human rights and freedoms.[118] Professionals have indicated a lack of trust in AI and an unease about its accuracy.[119]

The international regulatory response to AI has ranged from voluntary commitments (including from AI companies) to mandatory legislated obligations. In November 2023 the Bletchley Declaration was signed by 28 countries with the intention of greater international cooperation in managing the challenges and risks of AI. The European Union's Artificial Intelligence Act adopts a risk-based approach for quality assurance testing prior to the deployment of high-risk AI systems and also during

[115] S El Achkar, *Quality Education for All? We need (more) teachers!*, International Labour Organization, (5 October 2023).

[116] Thomson Reuters, *Future of Professionals Report – How AI is the Catalyst for Transforming Every Aspect of Work*, (2023), 4.

[117] L. Loble, & A. Hawcroft, (2022). *Shaping AI and Edtech to Tackle Australia's Learning Divide.* University of Technology Sydney, 8.

[118] UNESCO, *UNESCO's* Recommendation *on the Ethics of Artificial Intelligence – Adopted on 23 November 2021*, (2023), 4. See also UNESCO, *Readiness Assessment Methodology: A Tool of the Recommendation on the Ethics of Artificial Intelligence*, (2023) and UNESCO, *Ethical Impact Assessment: A Tool of the Recommendation on the Ethics of Artificial Intelligence*, (2023).

[119] Thomson Reuters, *Future of Professionals Report – How AI is the Catalyst for Transforming Every Aspect of Work*, (2023), 30.

their lifecycle. AI systems in education are high-risk and will require registration in an EU database and be required to comply with mandatory obligations regarding quality, transparency, human supervision and security. On 30 October 2023 the United States President issued an Executive Order to establish new standards for AI safety and security and to provide privacy protection regarding its use.

The United Nations has noted that policies for AI in education: [120]

> need to go beyond the application of AI in educational contexts, to include all the connections between AI and education. In particular, this means teaching how AI works and how it might be created, and about the wider implications that AI has for local and global society.

However, "reaching an equilibrium between technological integration in learning spaces, while mitigating the harms of those same technologies is a difficult task".[121] The implementation of formal policies and guidance to date regarding AI has been slow and low.[122] In the education of school students, the Australian Framework for Generative Artificial Intelligence[123] seeks to promote the responsible and ethical use of AI through six principles and 25 guiding statements:

1. Teaching and Learning – AI should be used to support and enhance teaching and learning
2. Human and Social Wellbeing – AI should be used to benefit all members of the school community
3. Transparency – School communities should understand how AI tools work, how they can be used, and when and how these tools are impacting on them

[120] UNESCO, *AI and education: Guidance for policy-makers*, (2021), 31

[121] L. Finlay, Australian Human Rights Commissioner, *Utilising Ethical AI in the Australian Education System*, Australian Human Rights Commission, Submission to the Standing Committee on Employment, Education and Training, (July 2023) Foreword.

[122] UNESCO, *UNESCO's Recommendations on the Ethics of Artificial Intelligence: Key Facts* (2023), 14, fewer than 10% of 450 schools and universities surveyed had organisational policies or guidelines regarding AI applications. See also E. Okagbue & Ors, *A comprehensive comprehensive overview of artificial intelligence and machine learning in education pedagogy: 21 Years (2000–2021) of research indexed in the scopus database*, (2023) 8 Social Sciences & Humanities, 1, 11.

[123] Commonwealth of Australia, *Australian Framework for Generative Artificial Intelligence*, (2023); see also European Union, *Ethical Guidelines on the use of artificial intelligence (AI) and data in teaching and learning for Educators*, (2022).

4. Fairness – AI tools should be used in ways that are accessible, fair and respectful
5. Accountability – AI tools should be open to challenge and retain human agency and accountability for decisions
6. Privacy, Security and Safety – Students and others using AI tools should have their privacy and data protected

In the development of specific policies for assignments and taught courses, teachers and educational institutions are encouraged to consider a three-stage approach:[124]

- **prohibiting the use of AI** where it interferes with the student developing foundational understanding, skills, and knowledge needed for future courses and careers
- **allowing the use of AI with attribution** where it could be a useful resource, but the teacher needs to be aware of its use by the student and the student must learn to take responsibility for accuracy and correct attribution of AI-generated content.
- **encouraging the use of AI and its active integration** into the learning process where students can leverage AI to focus on higher-level learning objectives, explore creative ideas, or otherwise enhance learning

Accordingly, whilst the regulatory landscape is changing very fast, compliance with standards (see also Chapter 3.2), organisational policies and regulatory requirements will continue to be vital for teaching professionals. Training and ongoing professional development are key to the effective use of technology, including AI. Neatly expressed:[125]

> AI is causing and will continue to instigate an onslaught of new training and development requirements - from basic training on how to make best use of AI to the need for upskilling and reskilling of existing professionals as well as changes to how junior professionals are educated on the job and within higher education.

When appropriate assessments have been made and the proposed technologies are suitable and compliant with all regulatory requirements, human-centric technology use (including AI) can provide numerous potential benefits to both student and teacher:

---

[124] Cornell University, *Generative Artificial Intelligence for Education and Pedagogy*, (July 2023).
[125] Thomson Reuters, *Future of Professionals Report – How AI is the Catalyst for Transforming Every Aspect of Work*, (2023), 21.

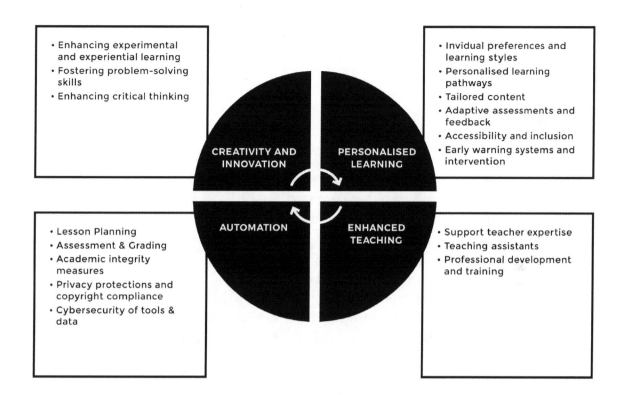

- Enhancing experimental and experiential learning
- Fostering problem-solving skills
- Enhancing critical thinking

- Invidual preferences and learning styles
- Personalised learning pathways
- Tailored content
- Adaptive assessments and feedback
- Accessibility and inclusion
- Early warning systems and intervention

CREATIVITY AND INNOVATION

PERSONALISED LEARNING

AUTOMATION

ENHANCED TEACHING

- Lesson Planning
- Assessment & Grading
- Academic integrity measures
- Privacy protections and copyright compliance
- Cybersecurity of tools & data

- Support teacher expertise
- Teaching assistants
- Professional development and training

Figure 9.2 Human-centric technology use (including AI) methodologies

9.4. Technology and Perspective

Technology itself transforms and disrupts. In a learning environment, this can be unsettling and distracting. Overenthusiasm for technology can sometimes be isolating, divisive, counterproductive, and expensive. Not everyone, teacher or student, is technology or computer literate. There is, and remains, a digital divide. Badly handled, adverse outcomes involving technology can result.

However, properly applied, technology has the capacity to inspire, motivate, and lead to discovery moments. It can also increase equity and accessibility. It can enable more personalised learning and assessment, expedite assessment results and their feedback, and improve the quality of the learning experience. Ultimately and pragmatically for the digital age, technology-awareness and competence is a necessary skill and is inherent in the modern learning environment. With its advantages and disadvantages, the use of technology therefore requires perspective. Its implementation requires consideration of both the teacher's and the student's points of view. Beyond relevance to the course or programme, considerations about technology (and its choices) include questions of financial capacity, competence, and the endurance of the skills taught and sought to be learnt.

9.5. Implementing Technology

Careful planning is required before implementing technology. Around the world, there are specialist education designers committed to technology enhanced learning (TEL) who guide, assist, and improve the implementation of technology in the classroom. Their tools, like the technologies they employ, are diverse; illuminating; and, often memorable when put into practice.

The use and implementation of technology should be considered and scholarly, rather than simply technology-driven and just technical training.[126] In making assessments about the choice of technology and the manner of its implementation, there are a number of useful models[127] or frameworks.[128] Ultimately, due to their cost and their enterprise-wide implications, decisions about technology will often be made at an institutional level. Technology will only be introduced, or introduced further, where it is perceived to satisfy one of the following purposes:

1. enhancing the course or teaching materials
2. enabling the accommodation of diverse learning styles
3. increasing student motivation
4. improving learning outcomes.

Each of these purposes has significant subjectivity. Evidence-based results are often difficult to discern prior to the introduction of a new technology, let alone upon its use. It has been said, pithily, "If a teacher uses PowerPoint or a video-enhanced podcast to deliver a lecture, it does not make it anything other than a lecture. Technology might make the lecture accessible to learners

---

[126] A. Kirkwood and L. Price, "Missing: Evidence of a Scholarly Approach to Teaching and Learning with Technology in Higher Education", *Teaching in Higher Education*, 18 (2013), 327.

[127] Puentedura's "SAMR" model (substitution – augmentation – modification – redefinition) was developed in 2003 to plan and assess the use of technologies in the classroom and is relatively straightforward and highly popular. However, Green has challenged the depth of its research. L. Green, "Through the Looking Glass: Examining Technology Integration in School Librarianship", *Knowledge Quest*, 43 (2014), 36.

[128] P. Mishra and M. Koehler, "108 Technological Pedagogical Content Knowledge: A Framework for Integrating Technology in Teachers' Knowledge", *Teachers College Record* (2006), 1,017. Mishra and Koehler developed the TPACK framework—TK (technical knowledge), PK (pedagogical knowledge), CK (content knowledge).

'anytime, anywhere,' but does not change it into something different."[129] Readiness and ethical impact assessments should be made prior to the introduction of technologies, including AI.[130]

The digital classroom will continue to become more technology rich. Together with technological competence, teaching professionals themselves will be encouraged to design, innovate, implement, and reflect on technology in their classroom. A human-centric approach will be more likely to align with the expectations of both the community and students. In the context of the use of AI, an insightful, interdisciplinary and collaborative approach is recommended:

> ..so much of how we interact with generative AI tooling will be rooted in prompt engineering and prompt design. .. asking technology the question in the right way, so that you get the best answer to resolve the problem statement that you're examining.[131]

9.6. The CAISSEP Technique for Teaching and Technology

This book, and its CAISSEP technique, seeks to identify effective teaching and learning methodologies for teaching professionals. It is, by design, able to be used, and reflected upon, in all teaching environments. Whenever technology is to be used, its role in the teaching environment should always seek to enhance the teaching and learning experience for the learner and the teacher. The relationship is symbiotic, complex and fragile – a true ecosystem. The role of technology (including AI) presents both opportunities and threats in the teaching environment and in society.

Experience tells us that it is often from our students that teachers learn the most. This is also true with technology, including AI. Students are often more advanced in the use of, and more interested in, modern technologies. Tapping into this interest and enthusiasm is invaluable to a mutual teaching and learning experience. By asking students about their interests in technology, with all its variants and the diverse tools available, promotes a human-centric approach to the use of technology. Key questions to ask yourself and your students can include:

1. Are you using technology (including AI) in your teaching?
2. Are your students using technology (including AI) in their learning?

---

[129] Kirkwood and L. Price, "Missing".

[130] UNESCO, *Readiness Assessment Methodology: A Tool of the Recommendation on the Ethics of Artificial Intelligence*, (2023) and UNESCO, *Ethical Impact Assessment: A Tool of the Recommendation on the Ethics of Artificial Intelligence*, (2023). Commonwealth of Australia, *Australian Framework for Generative Artificial Intelligence*, (2023).

[131] I Logvinova, *"Legal innovation and generative AI: Lawyers emerging as 'pilots', content creators and legal designers"*, ((2023), McKinsey & Company, In the Balance.

3. What are the potential benefits of using technology (including AI) in your teaching?
4. What are the potential benefits to students of using technology (including AI) in their learning?
5. What are the potential risks of using technology (including AI) in your teaching?
6. What are the potential risks to students of using technology (including AI) in their learning?
7. Will technology (including AI) assist my teaching?
8. Will technology (including AI) assist my students in their learning?
9. Will technology (including AI) be important in the future in your teaching?
10. Will technology (including AI) be important in the future for my students?

These questions can be readily used in any teaching environment by using the methodologies identified in Chapter 4. These methodologies can be applied using diverse technology (including AI) tools:

Description	Approach and Technology (including AI) Tools
Brainstorm	Free flow of ideas, which are noted and then discussed. Tools: Idea generation
Case study	Detailed consideration of an issue, often involving incremental learning, which can carry over more than one teaching period or seminar. Tools: Data analytics/ Predictive modelling
Group work	The seminar group itself is divided into groups. The groups collaborate on problem-solving for specific time periods, and then the problem and its solutions/issues are discussed by the whole seminar group. Tools: Collaborative problem-solving/ Group dynamics analysis
Intensity	Intense analysis of an issue or topic followed by more reflective discussion (can be in groups of two or more and can involve the merger or "snowball" of a small group into a larger group). Tools: Data visualisation/ Pattern recognition
Paper/project presentation	A paper or project prepared ahead of time is presented by a student (or group of students) and then discussed by the whole seminar group. Tools: Presentation design/ Content analysis
Poll	The tutor polls the class on an issue and, if there is divergence, students present differing perspectives. Tools: Polling analysis

Description	Approach and Technology (including AI) Tools
Questions and answers	Questions are identified by the tutor or seminar leader and students provide answers (individually or from their groups). Often these are best also written on whiteboards or captured using classroom technology for students to be able to note themselves and as a record of the seminar's discussion. Tools: Question and Answer platforms
Quizzes	Individual or group responses to a variety of set questions. Tools: Quiz generation
Role play / simulation	Students perform / act out roles based on factual or simulated situations and reflect on the issues. Tools: Simulated scenarios
Self-assessment	Individual tasks and exercises, which may then be brought back to the group for discussion and analysis Tools: Self-assessment tools/ Performance analytics
Warm-ups and Wind-downs	Activities at the commencement of a seminar (warm-ups) and at the end (wind-downs) can motivate increased participation in the seminar. They are an effective way to introduce new topics and to recap on the depth of understanding achieved. Tools: Engagement analytics

Figure 9.3 Teaching methodologies and technology (including AI) tools

By adopting, and reflecting on, the CAISSEP technique in the use of technology (including AI) and ensuring ongoing compliance with best practice standards and regulatory requirements, can be both enabling and re-assuring:

Technique	Emphasis	Style	CAISSEP for Teaching and Technology
CAISSEP. **CLARITY**	Easy to comprehend teaching and learning techniques that are readily apparent; distinctive; and explanatory of their content, tasks, and assessments	Clear, open, transparent, explanatory	❖ **Select teaching technology (including AI) clearly and consistently**

Technique	Emphasis	Style	CAISSEP for Teaching and Technology
CAISSEP. ANALYSIS	Active analytical investigation of problems, issues, and trends	Active, argument-based, experiential, solution-based and offering critical analysis, issue identification, advice, and judgement.	❖ **Ensure consistency in the use of technology (including AI)** ❖ **Design learning and discovery activities to include technology (including AI)**
CAISSEP. INQUIRY	Relevant inquisitive questioning based on self-directed learning and discovery	Autonomous, inquiring, eager for knowledge, involved.	❖ **Draw on student-based competence with technology (including AI)** ❖ **Draw on own experience with technology (including AI) in the design of teaching courses and materials** ❖ **Teach technology-based skills and methodologies (including AI) within taught courses**
CAISSEP. SYSTEM	Orderly provision of information and data based on principles, categories, and precedent	In-depth, detailed, informative, astute, discriminating	❖ **Identify relationships between teaching and technology (including AI)** ❖ **Include the most recent technology (including AI) and highlight technological change in teaching materials**

Technique	Emphasis	Style	CAISSEP for Teaching and Technology
C A I S S E P . **STRUCTURE**	Relevant, balanced, and logical consideration of issues by the use of consistent organised frameworks and methodical approaches	Reflective, analytical, organised, planned	❖ **Structure teaching and technology use (including AI) logically and consistently** ❖ **Use technology-based (including AI) frameworks**
C A I S S E P . **EMPHASIS**	Emphatic, focused, challenging, impactful	Clear highlighting of foundational issues, concepts and principles	❖ **Emphasise the value of teaching and its disruptive and transformative influences**
C A I S S E P . **PROFESSIONAL**	Emphasis on professional and ethical considerations integrated with reflective awareness	Professional, ethical, considered, fair, just, reflective	❖ **Professional approach to teaching and technology (including AI)** ❖ **Highlight the benefits and consequences of technology (including AI) in your discipline**

Figure 9.4 Teaching and technology methodologies

	Review of chapter 9 **Having read this chapter, you will be able to:**
1	Identify a teaching or learning experience that benefitted from the use of technology (including AI) and why it was beneficial
2	Identify three purposes for which technology (including AI) is introduced for teaching
3	Identify two components of a student-centric teaching and technology model
4	Describe two ways in which inquiry plays a role in the CAISSEP technique to enhance the teaching and technology (including AI) experience

CHAPTER 10

Conclusion: Learning More

*True teachers are those who use themselves as bridges over which they invite their students to cross;
then, having facilitated their crossing, joyfully collapse, encouraging them to create their own.*

—Nikos Kazantzakis

10.1. Teaching Is a Journey

Like this book, teaching is a journey. Each journey is one's own.[132] The teaching experience and its trials and tribulations are influenced by differing environments, individual choices, varying opportunities, and diverse abilities. This book is intended to guide as much as to challenge. It is intended to inform as much as to stimulate further reflection. It is intended to foster an enthusiasm to search for, and to communicate, knowledge. It is hoped that that it has been a bridge over which you have crossed and that it has inspired you to encourage your students to create their own.

Most of all, however, it is dedicated to students and to the classroom by providing methods, styles, and perspectives to aid you, the teacher. At its heart is the CAISSEP technique. As we progress, we can improve by applying the CAISSEP techniques in our ongoing professional development. These techniques can be used to prompt us or inspire us to "practice what we preach". Using a few simple examples:

- *Clarity.* Prepare a summary of your teaching technique that is clear, open, transparent, and self-explanatory.
- *Analyse.* Undertake a self-analysis of your teaching technique and styles

---

[132] See, for example, W. Prosser, "Lighthouse No Good", *Journal of Legal Education*, 1 (1948), 257.

- *Inquiry.* Undertake some self-directed learning and discovery that is of interest to you.
- *System.* Do a deep dive into a challenging, in-depth, more detailed programme.
- *Structure.* Identify a logical, reflective, planned approach to your courses or career; observe others as they teach; join a discussion group or routinely mentor others.
- *Emphasise.* Emphasise your own strengths and areas of expertise in your work
- *Professional.* Join a professional association and attend conferences or professional development programmes. Share your knowledge, and experience, with others.

Put simply, teaching requires passion, but it also requires determination and grit. It requires life experience, but it also requires the capacity and willingness to share, to listen and to learn. Teaching involves teams, individuals, and organisations; but it's not a sport. Teaching involves resources, management, and marketing; but it's not a corporation. Teaching involves, zeal, reflection, and belief; but it's not a religion. Teaching involves each of these things and more.

10.2. Teaching and Some of Its Motivations

This book commenced with a question about what motivates us to teach. Broadly, each of us has, at least, three influences—our own, our students' and the community's. Our own motivations are personal to each one of us. Our students' motivations are personal to them and influence us as we teach. Community motivations are influenced by the values and support of the community. Each requires sharing to ensure alignment to ensure that they are mutually beneficial. When this occurs, this can be described as the teaching "sweet spot", where a maximum teaching experience for all is achieved based on a given mutual effort. In doing so, student learning is maximised: "Our expectations of students, our interactions with them both inside and outside the classroom, and our enthusiasm for teaching them can greatly enhance or hinder their learning. Research from a variety of fields establishes beyond doubt the truth of these observations."[133]

10.3. Teaching, the Global Community, and the Adult Literacy Challenge

However, there is also a fourth influence—our role in the global community. This book commenced with an inspirational quote from Ana of Peru about the transformative effect of education. It identified, prior to the coronavirus pandemic, the pressing need for change in

---

[133] J. Levy, "As a Last Resort, Ask the Students: What They Say Makes Someone an Effective Law Teacher", *Maine Law Review*, 58 (2006), 50, 98.

relation to international adult literacy levels. Even with the devastating impacts of the coronavirus on communities and societies worldwide, we do have the capacity; we just need the will. With advancements in technology (including AI), we need to maintain both a human-centric and student-centric approach.

We all share a common future.[134] In a historic speech on 25 May 1961, then United States President John F. Kennedy proposed that, before that decade was out, it was the United States' goal that a human would land on Earth's moon and return safely to Earth. On 12 September 1962, President Kennedy was made an honorary visiting professor of Rice University in Houston, Texas. Upon receiving the award, the President gently and humorously reassured the estimated audience of 40,000 in Rice Stadium that his "first lecture will be very brief." Famously, he said:

> We choose to go to the Moon in this decade and do the other things, not because they are easy, but because they are hard; because that goal will serve to organize and measure the best of our energies and skills, because that challenge is one that we are willing to accept, one we are unwilling to postpone, and one we intend to win, and the others, too.

Approximately a year later, and on this occasion at American University in Washington DC, on 10 June 1963, President Kennedy spoke on a different topic—cherishing our children's future. "For, in the final analysis, our most basic common link is that we all inhabit this small planet. We all breathe the same air. We all cherish our children's future. And we are all mortal," he said.

On 20 July 1969, the Apollo 11 mission landed the first human on the moon and returned each of the three astronauts safely to Earth.

We have remarkable capacity, resilience, and drive.

To paraphrase President Kennedy, improving adult learning and literacy is not easy; rather, it's hard. It is a goal that will capture the best of our energies and skills. It's a challenge we should be willing to accept, unwilling to postpone, and committed to winning.

10.4. The Gift of Teaching

In conclusion, by teaching, we are given and give a gift. There is the gift of knowledge in our hands, together with the responsibility to share it; the gift of receiving from our students as they learn and discover with our assistance; the gift that, as we teach, we learn more about ourselves.

---

[134] World Commission on Environment and Development, *Our Common Future* (Oxford: OUP, 1987).

The CAISSEP technique is derived, in part, from the French and Latin words for box. Gifts are often traditionally given in boxes in many cultures around the world at various celebratory times of the year and on diverse memorable occasions. It is my genuine hope that the CAISSEP technique will be an enduring gift that enhances and inspires you, day by day, as you develop, reimagine, and renew your art of teaching.

In the words of Ana, a teacher from Lima, Peru: "Our responsibility as teachers is enormous, and our commitment to provide quality education must be renewed every day."[135]

C A I S S E P .

---

[135] UNESCO, *Teaching and Learning*.

BIBLIOGRAPHY

Archer, A., and Gleeson, M. *Skills for School Success* (Book 6) (Curriculum Associates, 1994).

Australian Trade and Investment Commission. "Australian Education Technology—Education of the Future Now" (Commonwealth of Australia, 2016).

Australian Government Office for Learning and Teaching, *Australian University Teaching Criteria and Standards Framework* (2020).

Bain, K. *What the Best College Teachers Do* (Harvard University Press, 2004).

Barnett, J. et al. "Clinical Supervision, Teaching, and Mentoring", *The Clinical Supervisor*, 20 (2002), 217.

Barrows, H., and Tamblyn R. *Problem-Based Learning: An Approach to Medical Education* (Springer, 1980).

Bates, A. *Teaching in a Digital Age* (Tony Bates Associates Ltd, 2015).

Bens, I. *Facilitating with Ease!* (San Francisco: John Wiley and Sons Inc, Jossey-Bass, 2012).

Berry, J. *Reclaiming the Ivory Tower: Organizing Adjuncts to Save Higher Education* (Monthly Review Press, 2005).

Biggs, J., and Tang, C. *Teaching for Quality Learning at University* (3rd edn, McGraw Hill, 2007).

Boud, D., and Feletti, G. *The Challenge of Problem-Based Learning* (London: Kogan Page, 2nd edn, 1997).

Boyer, E. *Scholarship Reconsidered: Priorities of the Professoriate* (The Carnegie Foundation for the Advancement of Teaching, 1990).

Boyle, R., and Dunn, R. "Teaching Law Students through Individual Learning Styles", *Alberta Law Review*, 62 (1998–1999), 213.

Bray, R. et al. "Effects of Group Size, Problem Difficulty, and Sex on Group Performance and Member Reactions", *Journal of Personality and Social Psychology*, 36 (1978), 1,224.

Brookfield, S. *Understanding and Facilitating Adult Learning* (Jossey-Bass, 1991).

Bruner, R. "Repetition is the First Principle of All Learning", *Psychology* (2001).

Burris, R. et al. *Teaching Law with Computers: A Collection of Essays* (Routledge 1979).

Carr, D. *Professionalism and Ethics in Teaching* (Routledge, 1999).

Cheville, J. *Minding the Body—What Student Athletes Know about Learning* (Heinemann USA, 2001).

Clarke, V., and Braun, V. "Teaching Thematic Analysis: Overcoming Challenges and Developing Strategies for Effective Learning", *Psychologist*, 26 (2013), 120.

Clutterbuck, D. et al. *Mentoring and Diversity: An International Perspective* (Oxford, 2002).

Coates, H., et al. "Australia's Casual Approach to Its Academic Teaching Workforce", *People and Place*, 17 (2009), 47.

Commonwealth of Australia, *Australian Framework for Generative Artificial Intelligence*, (2023).

Commonwealth of Australia, *Safe and responsible AI in Australia consultation, Australian Government's interim response*, (2024).

Cornell University, *Generative Artificial Intelligence for Education and Pedagogy*, (July 2023).

Cutten, G. "The College Professor as Teacher" *School and Society*, 86 (1958), 372.

Dale, P. *Audiovisual Methods in Teaching* (3rd edn, Holt, Rinehart and Winston, 1969).

Davis, B. *Tools for Teaching* (Jossey-Bass Publishers, 1993).

Davis, G., and Owen, S. *Some Innovations in Assessment in Legal Education* (Council of Australian Law Deans, 2009).

Duch, B., Groh, S., and Allen, D., eds. *The Power of Problem-Based Learning* (Sterling, VA: Stylus, 2001).

Earle, L. *Assessment as Learning* (Thousand Oaks: Corwin Press, 2003).

El Achkar, S., *Quality Education for All? We need (more) teachers!*, International Labour Organization, (5 October 2023).

European Parliament, *Artificial intelligence act, Briefing*, (June 2023), 3.

European Union, *Ethical Guidelines on the use of artificial intelligence (AI) and data in teaching and learning for Educators*, (2022).

Fehring, H., and Rodrigues, S., eds. *Teaching, Coaching and Mentoring Adult Learners: Lessons for Professionalism and Partnership* (New York, NY: Routledge, 2017).

Finlay, L., Australian Human Rights Commissioner, *Utilising Ethical AI in the Australian Education System*, Australian Human Rights Commission, Submission to the Standing Committee on Employment, Education and Training, (July 2023) Foreword

Fisher, D., et al. *Content Area Strategies for Adolescent Literacy* (Pearson, 2007).

Fuller, L. "On Teaching Law" *Stanford Law Review*, 3 (1950–1951), 35.

Gibbs, G. *Learning by Doing* (Oxford Centre for Staff and Learning Development, 2013).

Gibbs, G. "Using Assessment Strategically to Change the Way Students Learn", in S. Brown and A. Glasner, eds. *Assessment Matters in Higher Education* (Open University Press, 1999).

Green, L. "Through the Looking Glass: Examining Technology Integration in School Librarianship", *Knowledge Quest*, 43 (2014), 36.

Greer, D. *Designing Teaching Strategies: An Applied Behaviour Analysis Systems Approach* (Academic Press: Elsevier Science, 2002).

Gomes, L., and Anselm, P. *Scaffolding Learning and Maximising Engagement*, https://learningandteaching-navitas.com/scaffolding-learning-maximising-engagement/.

Hargreaves, A., and Fullan, M. *"Mentoring in the New Millennium", Theory into Practice* (2000), 50.

Harrison, N and Sellwood J, *"Learning and Teaching in Aboriginal and Torres Strait Islander Education"* (Oxford University Press, 4th Edition, 2022), 93, 179.

Hativa, N. *Clarity in Teaching: Importance and Components, Teaching for Effective Learning in Higher Education* (Springer, 2000).

Hews, R., and Ors, "Creative confidence and thinking skills for lawyers: Making sense of design thinking pedagogy in legal education", *Thinking Skills and Creativity* (2023), 2.

Hmelo-Silver, C. "Problem-Based Learning: What and How Do Students Learn?" *Educational Psychology Review*, 16 (2004), 235.

Holloway, E. "Structures for the Analysis and Teaching of Supervision", in C. E. Watkins, Jr., ed., *Handbook of Psychotherapy Supervision* (John Wiley and Sons Inc., 1997), 249.

Honey, P., and Mumford, A. *The Manual of Learning Styles* (Peter Honey Associates, 1986).

Hooks, B. *Teaching to Transgress: Education as the Practice of Freedom* (Routledge, 1994).

Horowitz, I., and Bordens, K. "The Effects of Jury Size, Evidence Complexity and Note Taking on Jury Process and Performance in a Civil Trial", *Journal of Applied Psychology* (2002), 121.

Johnson, D., et al. "Cooperative Learning: Improving University Instruction by Basing Practice on Validated Theory", *Journal on Excellence in College Teaching*, 25 (2014), 85.

Kamler, B., and Thomson, P. *Helping Doctoral Students Write: Pedagogies for Supervision* (Routledge, 2006).

Karge, B., et al. "Effective Strategies for Engaging Adult Learners", *Journal of College Teaching and Learning*, 8 (2011), 53.

Kift, S., et al. *Excellence and Innovation in Legal Education* (Lexis Nexis Butterworths, 2011).

King, A. "Changing College Classrooms: New Teaching and Learning Strategies for an Increasingly Complex World", chapter 2 in D. Halpern, ed., *Inquiry as a Tool in Critical Thinking* (Jossey-Bass, 1994).

Kirkwood, A., and Price, L. "Missing: Evidence of a Scholarly Approach to Teaching and Learning with Technology in Higher Education", *Teaching in Higher Education*, 18 (2013), 327.

Knowles, M. *The Adult Learner: A Neglected Species* (Gulf Publishing Co, 1973).

Knowles, M. *The Adult Learner* (6th edn, New York: Elsevier, 2005).

Kolb, D. *Experiential Learning—Experience as the Source of Learning and Development* (New Jersey: Prentice-Hall, 1984).

Lakey, B. *Facilitating Group Learning: Strategies for Success with Adult Learners* (Jossey-Bass, 2010).

Lasso, R. "From the Paper Chase to the Digital Chase: Technology and the Challenge of Teaching 21st Century Law Students" *Santa Clara Law Review*, 43 (2002–2003), 1.

Leach, J., and Moon, B. *Learners and Pedagogy* (Paul Chapman Publishing, 1999).

Ledvinka, G. "Reflection and Assessment in Clinical Legal Education: Do You See What I See?" *International Journal of Clinical Legal Education* (2006), 29.

Levy, J. "As a Last Resort, Ask the Students: What They Say Makes Someone an Effective Law Teacher" *Maine Law Review*, 58 (2006), 50.

Loble, L., & Hawcroft, A., (2022). *Shaping AI and Edtech to Tackle Australia's Learning Divide*. University of Technology Sydney.

Logvinova, I, *"Legal innovation and generative AI: Lawyers emerging as 'pilots', content creators and legal designers"*, ((2023), McKinsey & Company, In the Balance

Lyman, F. "Think-Pair-Share: An Expanding Teaching Technique", *MAA-CIE Cooperative News*, 1 (1987).

Mager, R. *Preparing Instructional Objectives: A Critical Tool in the Development of Effective Instruction* (3rd edn, Center for Effective Performance, 1997).

Markham, F. *Oxford* (London: Weidenfeld and Nicolson, 1967).

Martin, F. "Teaching Legal Problem Solving: A Problem-Based Learning Approach Combined with a Computerised Generic Problem" *Legal Education Review* (2003), 77.

McGee, R. *Teaching the Mass Class* (2nd edn, Washington: American Sociological Association, 1991).

Mishra, P., and Koehler, M. "Technological Pedagogical Content Knowledge: A Framework for Integrating Technology in Teachers' Knowledge", *Teachers College Record*, 108 (2006), 1017.

Moore, W. *The Tutorial System and its Future* (Oxford: Pergamon Press, 1968).

Nehme, M. "The Nexus between Teaching and Research: Easier Said Than Done" *Legal Education Review*, 22/2 (2012), 241.

Norton, L. "Assessing Student Learning", in "A Handbook for Teaching and Learning", in H. Fry et al., *Higher Education: Enhancing Academic Practice* (3rd edn, Routledge, 2009).

OECD, *Assessment of Higher Education Learning Outcomes, Feasibility Study Report—Design and Implementation*, 1 (2012).

Okagbue, E. & Ors, *A comprehensive overview of artificial intelligence and machine learning in education pedagogy: 21 Years (2000–2021) of research indexed in the scopus database*, (2023) 8 *Social Sciences & Humanities*, 1, 11.

Palfreyman, D., ed. *The Oxford Tutorial* (Oxford: OxCHEPS, 2008).

Palmer, P. *The Courage to Teach—Exploring the Inner Landscape of the Teacher's Life* (Jossey-Bass, 2007).

Perkins, J. "Organization and Functions of the University", *The Journal of Higher Education*, 43/9, (1972), 679.

Phillips, E., and Pugh, D. *How to Get a PhD: A Handbook for Students and their Supervisors* (4th edn, Maidenhead, UK: Open University Press, 2005).

Prosser, W. "Lighthouse No Good", *Journal of Legal Education*, 1(1948), 257.

Quality Assurance Agency, *Code of Practice for the Assurance of Academic Quality and Standards in Higher Education* (2nd edn, 2006).

Ranzijn, R., et al. "Introduction to Cultural Competence", in *Psychology and Indigenous Australians: Foundations of cultural competence* (Palgrave/ Macmillan, 2009).

Renner, P. *The Art of Teaching Adults: How to Become an Exceptional Instructor & Facilitator* (Training Assoc. Ltd, 1993).

Rockwater v. *Technip France SA & Ors* [2004] EWCA Civ 381.

Roulston, C. "Supervising a Doctoral Student", *Teaching Politics and International Relations* (2012), 210.

Savery, J. "Overview of PBL: Definitions and Distinctions", *Interdisciplinary Journal of Problem-Based Learning*, (2006), 9.

Saville, K. "Strategies for Using Repetition as a Powerful Teaching Tool", *Music Educators Journal* 98 (2011), 69.

Schaps, E. "Creating a School Community", *Educational Leadership*, 60/6 (2003), 31.

Schwartz, S., and Karge, B. *Human Diversity: A Guide for Understanding* (New York: McGraw-Hill, 1996).

Sherwin, R, et al. "Law in the Digital Age: How Visual Communication Technologies are Transforming the Practice, Theory, and Teaching of Law", *B.U. J. Sci. & Tech. L.*, 12 (2006), 227.

Soboroff, S. "Group Size and the Trust, Cohesion, and Commitment of Group Members", PhD thesis, University of Iowa, 2012.

Squires, G., *Teaching as a Professional Discipline*, (Falmer Press, 1999)

Stewart, G. "A Meta-Analytic Review of Relationships between Team Design Features and Team Performance", *Journal of Management*, 32 (2006), 29.

Sullivan, W., et al. *Educating Lawyers* (San Francisco: Jossey-Bass, 2007).

Tait, G., et al. "Laughing with the Lecturer: The Use of Humour in Shaping University Teaching", *Journal of University Teaching & Learning Practice*, 1 (2015).

Thomson, D. *Law School 2.0: Legal Education for a Digital Age* (Lexis Nexis, 2009).

Thomson Reuters, *Future of Professionals Report – How AI is the Catalyst for Transforming Every Aspect of Work*, (2023), 4

Torp, L., and Sage, S. *Problems as Possibilities: Problem-Based learning for K-16 Education* (2nd edn, Alexandria, VA: Association for Supervision and Curriculum Development, 2002).

Trigwell, K., et al. "Scholarship of Teaching: A Model", *Higher Education Research and Development*, 19/2 (2000), 155.

Tuckman, B. "Developmental Sequence in Small Groups", *Psychological Bulletin*, 65 (1965), 384.

UNESCO, *AI and education: Guidance for policy-makers*, (2021), 31.

UNESCO, *Ethical Impact Assessment: A Tool of the Recommendation on the Ethics of Artificial Intelligence*, (2023).

UNESCO, *Readiness Assessment Methodology – A Tool of the Recommendation on the Ethics of Artificial Intelligence*, (2023), 5

UNESCO, *Teaching and Learning: Achieving quality for all - 11th Education for All Global Monitoring Report* (UNESCO, 2014)

UNESCO, *UNESCO's Recommendations on the Ethics of Artificial Intelligence: Key Facts* (2023), 14.

United Nations, *Education During COVID-19 and Beyond, Policy Brief* (August 2020)

Universities Australia. *National Best Practice Framework for Indigenous Cultural Competency in Australian Universities* (Canberra: Department of Education, Employment and Workplace Relations, 2011).

Vandepeer, C., *Applied Thinking for Intelligence Analysis: A Guide for Practitioners*, Commonwealth of Australia, (2014), 41-42.

Van Doren, M. *Liberal Education* (New York: Henry Holt, 1943).

Velmahos, G., et al. Cognitive Task Analysis for Teaching Technical Skills in an Inanimate Surgical Skills Laboratory", *The American Journal of Surgery*, 187 (2004), 114.

Wade, J. "Meet MIRAT: Legal Reasoning Fragmented into Learnable Chunks" *Legal Education Review*, 2 (1990–1991), 283.

Warner, R., et al. "Teaching Law with Computers", *Rutgers Computer & Tech. L.J.*, 24 (1998), 107.

Welsch, S. *Mentoring the Future: A Guide to Building Mentor Programs that Work* (Global Book, 2004).

Whaley, D. "Teaching Law: Advice for the New Professor", *Ohio St. L.J.*, 43 (1982), 125.

Wiggins, G., and McTighe, J. *Understanding by Design* (Association for Supervision and Curriculum Development, 1998).

Winkelmes, M. "Transparency in Teaching: Faculty Share Data and Improve Students' Learning", *Liberal Education*, 99 (2013), 2.

Wisker, G. *The Good Supervisor: Supervising Postgraduate and Undergraduate Research for Doctoral Theses and Dissertations* (New York: Palgrave Macmillan, 2005).

Wong, H., and Wong, R. *The First Days of School—How to Be an Effective Teacher* (5th edn, Harry K Wong Publications, Inc., 2018).

World Commission on Environment and Development, *Our Common Future* (Oxford: OUP, 1987).

Yousafzai, M., and Lamb, C. *I am Malala: The Girl Who Stood up for Education and Was Shot by the Taliban* (Little Brown and Company, 2013).

Ziller, R. "Group Size: A Determinant of the Quality and Stability of Group Decisions", *Sociometry*, 20 (1957), 165.

INDEX

Printed in the United States
by Baker & Taylor Publisher Services